PyTorch MASTERY

From·the Essential to the Exceptional

Ethan Westwood

SMART B O O K S

"Mastering deep learning with PyTorch is not just about learning a framework—it's about embracing a mindset of continuous innovation and problem-solving. I hope this book serves as both a practical guide and a source of inspiration. Your ability to apply these concepts will not only shape your success as an AI practitioner but also drive the future of intelligent systems."

- *Ethan Westwood*

3

Table of Contents

5

6

Preface

The field of deep learning has rapidly transformed industries, from healthcare and finance to autonomous systems and creative applications. As artificial intelligence continues to evolve, the demand for efficient, scalable, and user-friendly deep learning frameworks has never been greater. PyTorch has emerged as one of the leading frameworks, offering researchers and engineers the flexibility, speed, and ease of use required to build cutting-edge machine learning models.

When I first started exploring deep learning, I encountered a common challenge: the steep learning curve of implementing neural networks efficiently. While there were abundant theoretical resources available, practical implementation often seemed overwhelming due to the complexity of tools and frameworks. PyTorch changed this landscape by making deep learning more intuitive, providing dynamic computation graphs, automatic differentiation, and seamless GPU acceleration.

This book was born out of a desire to bridge the gap between deep learning theory and hands-on implementation. Whether you are a beginner taking your first steps into artificial intelligence or an experienced developer looking to refine your PyTorch skills, this book provides a structured, comprehensive guide to mastering deep learning with PyTorch. The content has been meticulously organized to ensure a smooth learning experience, starting from fundamental concepts and progressing to advanced techniques and real-world applications.

I invite you to explore this book not just as a reference but as a practical companion in your deep learning journey. The goal is to empower you with the confidence to build, train, and deploy powerful neural networks while understanding the inner workings of PyTorch. Let's embark on this journey together, transforming complex ideas into tangible, high-performing AI solutions.

Ethan Westwood

Introduction

Deep learning has revolutionized the field of artificial intelligence, enabling machines to perform tasks that were once thought to be exclusive to human intelligence. From natural language processing and computer vision to reinforcement learning and generative models, deep learning has become the foundation of modern AI-driven innovations.

At the heart of deep learning lies the need for efficient frameworks that allow researchers and engineers to build and experiment with complex models. PyTorch, developed by Facebook AI, has become one of the most widely adopted frameworks due to its ease of use, flexibility, and powerful capabilities. Unlike static frameworks that require predefined computation graphs, PyTorch allows for dynamic computation, making model building and debugging much more intuitive.

This book is designed to provide a deep and practical understanding of PyTorch, covering essential concepts and techniques needed to build state-of-the-art deep learning models. We will begin by introducing the fundamentals, such as tensors, automatic differentiation, and data handling, before moving on to neural network architectures, training strategies, and evaluation methods. We will also explore advanced topics, including computer vision, natural language processing, optimization techniques, and deploying models into production environments.

By the end of this book, you will not only have a strong grasp of PyTorch but also the ability to apply these concepts to real-world problems. Whether your goal is to develop AI-powered applications, conduct cutting-edge research, or optimize existing models for production, this book will equip you with the necessary skills to succeed.

Deep learning is a constantly evolving field, and learning never truly stops. I encourage you to experiment, contribute to the AI community, and push the boundaries of what is possible with PyTorch. Let's dive in and start building the future of AI, one model at a time.

Part 1: Foundations

Chapter 1: Introduction to PyTorch

1.1 What is PyTorch and Why Use It?

PyTorch is a powerful open-source deep learning framework developed by Facebook AI Research (FAIR). Since its release, it has become one of the most popular tools for both academic research and industry applications, thanks to its flexibility, ease of use, and dynamic computation graph. Unlike static frameworks that require defining the entire computation graph in advance, PyTorch allows dynamic computation, enabling users to modify models and experiment in real time. This feature is especially valuable for AI researchers and engineers working on cutting-edge innovations.

One of PyTorch's biggest advantages is its intuitive, Pythonic design. It integrates seamlessly with Python's scientific computing ecosystem, including libraries like NumPy and SciPy, making it easy for data scientists and machine learning practitioners to transition from traditional numerical computing to deep learning. PyTorch also provides native support for GPU acceleration, leveraging NVIDIA CUDA to significantly speed up model training and inference, which is crucial for handling large-scale datasets and complex architectures.

Beyond its technical strengths, PyTorch has built a thriving ecosystem and is widely adopted in both academia and industry. Many state-of-the-art AI models and research papers are implemented in PyTorch, reinforcing its credibility as a leading deep learning framework. Major companies, including Tesla, Meta (formerly Facebook), OpenAI, and Microsoft, rely on PyTorch for their AI-driven applications, demonstrating its robustness, scalability, and production-readiness. With an active community and continuous updates, PyTorch remains at the forefront of deep learning innovation.

1.1.1 Key Advantages of PyTorch

One of PyTorch's defining features is its dynamic computation graph, which sets it apart from static graph-based frameworks like TensorFlow 1.x. This flexibility allows developers to modify the computation graph on the fly, making it especially useful for debugging, experimentation, and research. With PyTorch, users can build complex models interactively, adjusting components as needed without being constrained by a predefined structure.

Another major advantage of PyTorch is its ease of use and Pythonic nature. Designed to feel intuitive for Python developers, PyTorch integrates seamlessly with widely used scientific computing libraries such as NumPy, Pandas, and SciPy. This makes the transition from traditional numerical computing to deep learning more natural, allowing data scientists and machine learning engineers to prototype and iterate quickly.

PyTorch also excels in GPU acceleration, providing built-in support for CUDA. This enables effortless deployment of models on GPUs, significantly boosting computation speed without requiring extensive boilerplate code. The framework's efficient handling of parallel computations makes it ideal for training large-scale deep learning models.

Beyond its core functionalities, PyTorch benefits from a rich ecosystem of specialized tools. Libraries such as TorchVision for computer vision, TorchText for natural language processing, and TorchAudio for audio-related tasks extend its capabilities, making it a versatile framework for a wide range of AI applications. Additionally, PyTorch's active community ensures continuous development, extensive documentation, and responsive support, fostering an environment that encourages innovation and collaboration.

PyTorch's widespread adoption in both research and industry further solidifies its position as a leading deep learning framework. Many state-of-the-art AI models are implemented using PyTorch, and major companies leverage it for real-world applications, including self-driving cars, recommendation systems, and medical imaging. Its combination of flexibility, performance, and ease of use has made PyTorch a preferred choice for cutting-edge artificial intelligence development.

1.2 Installation and Setup

Before using PyTorch, you need to install it on your system. PyTorch supports multiple installation methods, including direct installation via pip, conda, or from source. The recommended installation method depends on your operating system and whether you plan to use GPU acceleration.

1.2.1 Installing PyTorch with pip

For most users, installing PyTorch with `pip` is the easiest approach. Open a terminal and run:

```
Unset
pip install torch torchvision torchaudio
```

If you have an NVIDIA GPU and want to leverage CUDA for acceleration, you need to install the appropriate CUDA version. You can check the official PyTorch website for the latest compatible versions:

```
Unset
pip install torch torchvision torchaudio
--index-url
https://download.pytorch.org/whl/cu118
```

This installs PyTorch with CUDA 11.8 support. Make sure to adjust the version based on your system's CUDA capability.

1.2.2 Installing PyTorch with Conda

If you are using Anaconda, you can install PyTorch using the conda package manager:

```
Unset
conda install pytorch torchvision
torchaudio pytorch-cuda=11.8 -c pytorch -c
nvidia
```

This method ensures that all dependencies are managed properly, making it a preferred choice for many users.

1.2.3 Verifying Installation

To confirm that PyTorch is installed correctly, open a Python shell and run:

```Python
import torch

print(torch.__version__)

print(torch.cuda.is_available())  # Checks
if CUDA is available
```

If the output includes a valid PyTorch version and True for CUDA availability (assuming you installed the CUDA version), your setup is complete.

1.3 PyTorch vs. Other Frameworks

There are several deep learning frameworks available, each with its own strengths and weaknesses. Let's compare PyTorch with some of the most commonly used frameworks:

1.3.1 PyTorch vs. TensorFlow

TensorFlow, developed by Google, is another popular deep learning framework. While TensorFlow 1.x relied on static computation graphs, TensorFlow 2.x introduced dynamic computation through eager execution, making it more similar to PyTorch. However, PyTorch remains the preferred choice for researchers due to its ease of debugging and Pythonic nature. TensorFlow, on the other hand, excels in production environments due to its mature deployment tools, such as TensorFlow Serving and TensorFlow Lite.

1.3.2 PyTorch vs. Keras

Keras is a high-level deep learning API that originally worked on top of TensorFlow. It is designed to be easy to use and beginner-friendly, but it lacks the flexibility required for advanced research. PyTorch provides more control over model design and training, making it a better choice for cutting-edge research and custom architectures.

1.3.3 PyTorch vs. JAX

JAX, developed by Google, is gaining popularity for its speed and automatic differentiation capabilities. Unlike PyTorch, JAX focuses on just-in-time (JIT) compilation, enabling high-performance computations. While JAX is powerful, PyTorch has a more extensive ecosystem and better documentation, making it more accessible to a broader audience.

1.4 Basic Architecture and Components

Understanding PyTorch's core architecture is essential for leveraging its full potential. Some of the key components include:

1.4.1 Tensors

Tensors are the fundamental data structures in PyTorch, similar to NumPy arrays but with built-in support for GPU acceleration. PyTorch tensors allow automatic differentiation, which is crucial for deep learning.

1.4.2 Autograd

PyTorch's `autograd` module enables automatic differentiation, allowing gradients to be computed efficiently. This is essential for training neural networks using backpropagation.

Modules and nn.Module

PyTorch provides an object-oriented approach to building neural networks through the `nn.Module` class. This class allows users to define and reuse network components in a structured manner.

1.4.3 Optimizers

The `torch.optim` module provides various optimization algorithms such as Stochastic Gradient Descent (SGD) and Adam, making it easy to train deep learning models.

1.4.4 Data Handling (Dataset and DataLoader)

PyTorch's `torch.utils.data` module provides classes like `Dataset` and `DataLoader`, which help in efficient data handling, batch processing, and augmentation.

1.5 Development Environment Setup

To ensure a smooth PyTorch development experience, consider setting up a well-structured environment.

1.5.1 Using Jupyter Notebooks

Jupyter Notebooks are highly recommended for interactive development, especially for experimenting with PyTorch. Install Jupyter with:

```Python
pip install notebook
```

Then, launch it with:

```Python
jupyter notebook
```

1.5.2 Using VS Code or PyCharm

For larger projects, a robust IDE like Visual Studio Code (VS Code) or PyCharm is recommended. These IDEs provide excellent debugging, syntax highlighting, and plugin support for PyTorch development.

1.5.3 Managing Virtual Environments

It's a good practice to use virtual environments to manage dependencies. You can create and activate a virtual environment using:

```
Python
python -m venv pytorch_env

source  pytorch_env/bin/activate     #  On
macOS/Linux

pytorch_env\Scripts\activate  # On Windows
```

This ensures that your PyTorch installation remains isolated from other projects.

Chapter 2: PyTorch Basics

Introduction

Before diving into the complexities of deep learning models, it is essential to establish a strong understanding of the core building blocks that power PyTorch. Deep learning frameworks like PyTorch are designed to facilitate the efficient construction, training, and deployment of neural networks, but without a firm grasp of the underlying components, it can be challenging to leverage their full potential effectively.

At its core, PyTorch is built around three fundamental concepts: **tensors**, **automatic differentiation (autograd)**, and **GPU-accelerated computation**. These components work together to provide a flexible and efficient environment for developing machine learning models. Tensors are the primary data structure in PyTorch, enabling mathematical operations and serving as the foundation for representing model parameters, inputs, and outputs. The automatic differentiation engine (autograd) tracks computations and dynamically constructs computational graphs, allowing gradients to be computed effortlessly during backpropagation—a crucial step in training neural networks. Finally, PyTorch's seamless integration with

GPUs provides the computational power necessary to train large-scale models efficiently.

In this chapter, we will systematically explore these foundational concepts, breaking them down into comprehensible sections. We will begin with an in-depth look at **tensors**, understanding their properties, types, and how they enable mathematical operations. Then, we will delve into **autograd**, examining how PyTorch automatically computes gradients and enables efficient model training. Next, we will discuss the principles of **gradient computation**, which form the basis for optimization techniques used in neural networks. Moving forward, we will introduce **basic neural network structures**, demonstrating how PyTorch provides tools for defining and implementing these models. Finally, we will explore **GPU acceleration**, highlighting how PyTorch leverages hardware capabilities to speed up deep learning computations.

By the end of this chapter, you will have a solid grasp of the essential mechanisms that drive deep learning in PyTorch. This foundational knowledge will not only make it easier to construct neural networks but will also provide you with the necessary intuition to optimize models, debug potential issues, and take full advantage of PyTorch's flexibility. With these fundamentals in place, you will be well-equipped to progress to more advanced topics, including efficient data handling, building deep learning architectures, and training large-scale models with PyTorch.

2.1 Tensors and Operations

2.1.1 What Are Tensors?

Tensors are the fundamental data structure in PyTorch, serving as the backbone for all computations in deep learning. They are **multidimensional arrays**, similar to NumPy arrays, but come with additional functionalities tailored for deep learning. These include **automatic differentiation** for gradient computation and **seamless GPU acceleration**, enabling high-performance computing.

In essence, tensors are generalizations of scalars, vectors, and matrices, extending to any number of dimensions. For example:

- A **scalar** is a single numerical value (0D tensor).

- A **vector** is a one-dimensional array of numbers (1D tensor).

- A **matrix** is a two-dimensional array (2D tensor).

- A **higher-dimensional tensor** (3D, 4D, or more) represents more complex data structures, such as images, video sequences, or batches of data.

Tensors form the core data structure in PyTorch because they provide the necessary flexibility and computational efficiency for handling large-scale machine learning tasks. The ability to perform operations on tensors efficiently, particularly using GPU acceleration, is one of PyTorch's greatest strengths.

2.1.2 Why Are Tensors Important in Deep Learning?

Deep learning models primarily deal with numerical data, whether it be **images, text, audio, or sensor readings**. These inputs, parameters, and outputs are all represented as tensors. For example:

- **Image data**: A grayscale image (height × width) can be represented as a 2D tensor, while an RGB image (height × width × color channels) is a 3D tensor.

- **Text data**: Sentences can be tokenized and converted into sequences of word embeddings, represented as 2D tensors (batch_size × embedding_dim).

- **Audio data**: Audio waveforms are typically stored as 1D tensors, while spectrograms can be represented as 2D tensors.

- **Batch processing**: When training deep learning models, multiple input samples are grouped together into **batches**, leading to 4D or even 5D tensors depending on the type of data being processed.

Efficiently handling and manipulating these tensors is critical for training machine learning models, as they define how inputs are processed, transformed, and passed through neural networks.

2.1.3 Creating Tensors in PyTorch

PyTorch provides multiple ways to create tensors, making it easy to initialize them for various use cases. Below are some of the most common methods:

1. Creating Tensors from Lists or NumPy Arrays

You can create a PyTorch tensor directly from a Python list or NumPy array:

```Python
import torch
```

```python
import numpy as np

# Creating a tensor from a Python list

tensor_from_list = torch.tensor([1, 2, 3,
4, 5])

# Creating a tensor from a NumPy array

numpy_array = np.array([6, 7, 8, 9, 10])

tensor_from_numpy                    =
torch.tensor(numpy_array)

print(tensor_from_list)

print(tensor_from_numpy)
```

PyTorch automatically infers the data type, but you can explicitly specify it using dtype:

```python
Python
float_tensor  =  torch.tensor([1.0,  2.0,
3.0], dtype=torch.float32)

int_tensor  =  torch.tensor([1,  2,  3],
dtype=torch.int32)
```

2. Creating Tensors with Default Initialization

PyTorch provides functions to create tensors initialized with common values:

```python
# Creating a tensor filled with zeros

zero_tensor = torch.zeros((3, 3))

# Creating a tensor filled with ones

ones_tensor = torch.ones((2, 2))

# Creating an identity matrix

identity_tensor = torch.eye(3)

# Creating a tensor with random values
(uniform distribution)

random_tensor = torch.rand((4, 4))

# Creating a tensor with normally
distributed values (mean=0, std=1)

normal_tensor = torch.randn((2, 2))

print(zero_tensor)

print(ones_tensor)
```

```python
print(identity_tensor)

print(random_tensor)

print(normal_tensor)
```

These functions are particularly useful when initializing weights in neural networks.

3. Creating Tensors with Specific Ranges and Shapes

PyTorch also provides functions for creating tensors with values from specific numerical ranges:

```python
Python
# Creating a tensor with values ranging
from 0 to 9

range_tensor = torch.arange(10)

# Creating a tensor with values spaced
evenly between 0 and 1

linspace_tensor = torch.linspace(0, 1,
steps=5)
```

```python
# Creating a tensor with logarithmically
spaced values

logspace_tensor = torch.logspace(1, 2,
steps=5)

print(range_tensor)

print(linspace_tensor)

print(logspace_tensor)
```

4. Creating Tensors Based on Another Tensor

Sometimes, you may want to create a new tensor with the same shape or properties as an existing tensor:

```python
Python
existing_tensor = torch.rand((3, 3))

# Creating a new tensor with the same
shape as an existing tensor

same_shape_tensor                        =
torch.zeros_like(existing_tensor)
```

```python
# Creating a new tensor with ones and the
same shape as another tensor

ones_like_tensor                       =
torch.ones_like(existing_tensor)

print(same_shape_tensor)

print(ones_like_tensor)
```

This approach is useful when defining weight matrices for models, ensuring they have compatible shapes.

2.1.4 Tensor Properties

Every tensor in PyTorch has key properties that define its behavior:

```python
Python
tensor = torch.rand((3, 4))

# Shape (number of elements along each
dimension)

print(tensor.shape)

# Number of dimensions
```

```
print(tensor.ndimension())

# Data type

print(tensor.dtype)

# Device (CPU or GPU)

print(tensor.device)
```

Understanding these properties is essential for debugging and optimizing tensor operations.

2.1.5 Tensor Operations

Tensors support a wide variety of operations, including:

- **Arithmetic operations**: Addition (+), subtraction (-), multiplication (*), division (/).

- **Matrix operations**: Dot product (torch.dot()), matrix multiplication (torch.matmul() or @ operator).

- **Indexing and slicing**: Similar to NumPy (tensor[0:2, 1:3]).

- **Reshaping tensors**: Using `.view()` or `.reshape()` to change dimensions.

Example:

```Python
a = torch.tensor([[1, 2], [3, 4]])

b = torch.tensor([[5, 6], [7, 8]])

# Element-wise addition

print(a + b)

# Matrix multiplication

print(torch.matmul(a, b))

# Reshaping a tensor

reshaped = a.view(1, 4)  # Reshape to (1, 4)

print(reshaped)
```

2.1.6 Moving Tensors Between CPU and GPU

One of PyTorch's major advantages is its **seamless GPU acceleration**. You can easily move tensors between CPU and GPU:

```python
device = torch.device("cuda" if
torch.cuda.is_available() else "cpu")

# Create a tensor on CPU

tensor_cpu = torch.tensor([1, 2, 3])

# Move it to GPU

tensor_gpu = tensor_cpu.to(device)

print(tensor_gpu.device)  # Output: cuda
if GPU is available
```

GPU acceleration dramatically speeds up deep learning computations, making it essential for training large-scale models.

Tensors are at the heart of PyTorch, enabling the representation and manipulation of data in an efficient manner. Unlike traditional NumPy arrays, PyTorch tensors come with built-in support for automatic differentiation and GPU acceleration, making them indispensable for deep learning. In this section, we explored tensor creation, properties, operations, and GPU integration, all of which lay the groundwork for building and training neural networks.

In the next section, we will explore **PyTorch's automatic differentiation mechanism (autograd)**, which enables seamless gradient computation for optimizing deep learning models.

2.2 Autograd Mechanism

2.2.1 Understanding Automatic Differentiation

The **autograd mechanism** is one of the most powerful features of PyTorch, allowing for the automatic computation of gradients. It is an essential component for training deep learning models, especially those that use **gradient-based optimization algorithms** such as **Stochastic Gradient Descent (SGD)**. The ability to compute gradients automatically is what enables the **backpropagation** algorithm, which is the cornerstone of training neural networks. Without automatic differentiation, the task of computing gradients for large, complex models would become incredibly difficult and time-consuming.

In this section, we will explore the concept of **automatic differentiation**, explain how it works in PyTorch, and look at how PyTorch tracks operations and computes gradients during backpropagation.

Automatic differentiation (autodiff) is a technique used to compute the derivative (gradient) of a function with respect to its inputs, automatically and efficiently, by breaking the function into a sequence of elementary operations. Unlike numerical differentiation, which approximates the derivative, and symbolic differentiation, which involves computing algebraic expressions for derivatives, automatic differentiation computes the gradient to **machine precision** by recording every operation in a computational graph.

In the context of deep learning, the goal is to compute the gradients of the loss function with respect to the model parameters (weights and biases) so that we can update them to minimize the loss. Autograd in PyTorch automates this process.

2.2.2 Computational Graphs and Backpropagation

At the heart of the autograd mechanism is the **computational graph**, which is essentially a directed acyclic graph (DAG) where each node represents an operation (e.g., addition, multiplication, activation function), and the edges represent the flow of data (tensors). This graph is constructed dynamically as operations are performed on tensors that require gradients.

In the training process, PyTorch records the sequence of operations for each tensor with the attribute `requires_grad=True`. Once the forward pass is completed and the loss is computed, PyTorch can use the computational graph to perform **backpropagation** and compute gradients.

How Backpropagation Works:

1. **Forward Pass**: During the forward pass, tensors are passed through the neural network, and various operations are performed. The results of these operations are stored in the computational graph. At each step, the function `requires_grad=True` tracks and records the operations performed on the tensor.

2. **Loss Calculation**: After performing the forward pass, we compute the loss, which is a scalar value that quantifies the error between the model's predictions and the true targets.

3. **Backward Pass**: Once the loss is calculated, the `backward()` method is called on the loss tensor. This method triggers backpropagation, where PyTorch traverses the computational graph in reverse order (from the output back to the input)

43

and computes the gradient of the loss with respect to each tensor.

4. **Gradient Computation**: PyTorch computes the gradient (derivative) of the loss with respect to the model's parameters (weights and biases) using the chain rule of calculus. The gradients are stored in the `.grad` attribute of the tensors that required gradients.

5. **Parameter Update**: After gradients are computed, optimization algorithms like **SGD** or **Adam** can be used to update the model parameters and minimize the loss.

2.2.3 `requires_grad` Attribute

The key to enabling autograd in PyTorch is the `requires_grad` attribute. This attribute determines whether PyTorch should track operations on the tensor for the purpose of gradient computation. By default, `requires_grad` is set to `False`, but we can set it to `True` to indicate that gradients should be calculated for this tensor.

How to Enable `requires_grad`:

```python
Python
import torch

# Create a tensor with requires_grad=True

x   =   torch.tensor([2.0,   3.0,   4.0],
requires_grad=True)

# Perform some operations

y = x * 2

# Print the computational graph status

print(x.requires_grad)   # True

print(y.requires_grad)   # True

# Compute the gradients by calling
backward() on a scalar output

y.sum().backward()   # Compute the sum of y
and perform backpropagation

# Print gradients of x

print(x.grad)
```

In this example, x is created with requires_grad=True, and when we perform operations on x, PyTorch keeps track of them in the computational graph. When `y.sum().backward()` is called, PyTorch computes the gradient of the sum of y with respect to x and stores the result in `x.grad`.

2.2.4 Gradient Computation and the `.grad` Attribute

Once backpropagation is performed, the computed gradients are stored in the `.grad` attribute of the tensor. This attribute holds the gradients of the tensor with respect to the loss.

For example, consider the following code:

```Python
import torch

# Create a tensor with requires_grad=True

x   =   torch.tensor([1.0,   2.0,   3.0],
requires_grad=True)

# Perform an operation

y = x ** 2 + 3 * x + 1
```

```
# Compute the sum and perform
backpropagation

y.sum().backward()

# Print the gradients

print(x.grad)  # Output: tensor([5.0, 7.0,
9.0])
```

In this case, the gradient of the loss with respect to x (i.e., dy/dx) is computed, and the result is stored in `x.grad`. These gradients represent how much each element of x influences the final loss, and they will be used by an optimizer to update the parameters.

2.2.5 Disabling Gradient Tracking with `torch.no_grad()`

While you typically want PyTorch to track gradients during training, there are times when you want to disable gradient tracking—for instance, during evaluation or inference when you do not need to compute gradients. PyTorch provides a context manager `torch.no_grad()` for this purpose.

For example:

```python
Python
import torch

# Disable gradient tracking

with torch.no_grad():

    x = torch.tensor([1.0, 2.0, 3.0],
requires_grad=True)

    y = x * 2

    print(y.requires_grad)  # False, as
gradients are not tracked inside the
no_grad context
```

This not only saves memory but also speeds up computations during inference since PyTorch does not need to keep track of the operations.

2.2.6 In-Place Operations and Their Impact on Autograd

PyTorch supports **in-place operations**, where an operation modifies the content of a tensor directly instead of creating a new tensor. These in-place operations are indicated by a trailing underscore (_) in their names, such as add_(), mul_(), and zero_().

However, in-place operations can interfere with the autograd mechanism because they may overwrite data needed for gradient computation. For example:

```python
x = torch.tensor([2.0, 3.0], requires_grad=True)

y = x * 2

# In-place operation

y.add_(1)  # This modifies y in place

# Backpropagation

y.sum().backward()

print(x.grad)  # This may give an error or incorrect result in some cases
```

It's important to be cautious when using in-place operations during training, as they can lead to incorrect gradients or errors in backpropagation.

2.2.7 Gradient Accumulation

When performing backpropagation, gradients are **accumulated** in the .grad attribute of the tensor. This is useful when working with **mini-batch training**, where the model's weights are updated after accumulating gradients from multiple forward-backward passes.

To reset the gradients before the next backward pass, you can use the `optimizer.zero_grad()` method:

```Python
optimizer = torch.optim.SGD([x], lr=0.01)

# Zero the gradients before performing the
backward pass

optimizer.zero_grad()

# Perform the forward pass, compute
gradients, and update parameters

loss = some_loss_function(x)

loss.backward()

# Perform parameter update

optimizer.step()
```

This is crucial to avoid **gradient accumulation** between iterations and ensure that the model's gradients are correctly updated during training.

2.3 Computing Gradients

In deep learning, the process of **computing gradients** is crucial for optimizing the model parameters (weights and biases) using gradient-based optimization methods like **Stochastic Gradient Descent (SGD)**. In PyTorch, the **autograd** mechanism takes care of computing these gradients during the **backpropagation** phase, which occurs after the forward pass. The gradients represent the rate of change of the loss function with respect to each parameter in the model.

Let's delve into the mechanics of how gradients are computed in PyTorch, starting with the **chain rule** and exploring how backpropagation works at a more detailed level.

2.3.1 The Chain Rule of Calculus and Backpropagation

At the core of gradient computation lies the **chain rule of calculus**, which allows us to compute the derivative of a function composed of multiple nested functions. In deep learning, the loss function is often a complex composition of many functions and operations (e.g., matrix multiplication, activation functions, etc.), so the chain rule helps break this down into simpler parts.

51

In simple terms, if we have a composite function:

$$z = f(g(x))$$

The chain rule tells us that the derivative of z with respect to x is the product of the derivative of f with respect to $g(x)$ and the derivative of g with respect to x:

$$\frac{dx}{dz} = \frac{dg}{dz} \cdot \frac{dx}{dg}$$

For neural networks, backpropagation applies this chain rule to compute the gradients of the loss with respect to each weight and bias in the network. The gradients tell us how much each parameter should change in order to minimize the loss.

2.3.2 Performing Backpropagation in PyTorch

Once a forward pass is completed, the **loss** (often a scalar value) is computed. The next step is to calculate the gradients by performing **backpropagation** using the `backward()` function on the loss tensor. Let's walk through a simple example to understand how backpropagation works in PyTorch.

Example: Simple Gradient Computation

```python
Python
import torch

# Create a tensor with requires_grad=True
to track operations on it

x = torch.tensor([2.0, 3.0],
requires_grad=True)

# Perform a simple operation (y = x^2 +
3x)

y = x**2 + 3*x

# Compute the sum of y (as a scalar)

z = y.sum()

# Perform backpropagation

z.backward()

# Print the gradients of x

print(x.grad)
```

In this example, the tensor x has `requires_grad=True`, meaning PyTorch will track operations involving x. The operation `y = x^2 + 3x` creates a computational graph. After computing the sum of `y` (`z = y.sum()`), we call `z.backward()` to calculate the gradients. PyTorch computes the gradient of `z` with respect to `x`, and the result is stored in `x.grad`.

Gradients Calculation:

To understand the gradients being computed here, let's break it down:

The function we are differentiating is:

$$z = \sum_i (x_i^2 + 3x_i)$$

Where x_i represents the individual elements of x The gradients of this with respect to each element of x are:

$$\frac{\partial z}{\partial x_i} = 2x_i + 3$$

For `x = [2.0, 3.0]`, the gradients would be:

$$\frac{\partial z}{\partial x_i} = 2(2.0) + 3 = 7$$

$$\frac{\partial z}{\partial x_i} = 2(3.0) + 3 = 9$$

Hence, the output of x.grad will be:

$$tensor([7.0, 9.0])$$

These are the gradients that will be used by the optimizer (like SGD) to update the parameters during the training process.

2.3.3 Higher-Order Gradients

Sometimes, you may need to compute **higher-order gradients**, such as the gradient of a gradient (i.e., second-order gradients). This is useful in advanced optimization techniques like **second-order optimization methods** or when implementing certain types of neural networks.

PyTorch allows the computation of higher-order gradients by setting `create_graph=True` when calling `backward()`:

```python
# Compute higher-order gradients (second
derivative)

y = x**3 + 2*x

y_sum = y.sum()

y_sum.backward(create_graph=True)

# Compute second-order gradients

z = x**2

z.backward()

print(x.grad)  # This will contain the
second-order gradients
```

By setting `create_graph=True`, PyTorch constructs the computational graph for the first-order gradients, which can later be used for calculating second-order gradients if needed.

2.3.4 Gradient Accumulation

In practice, especially when training large models, you often accumulate gradients over multiple forward-backward passes before performing a parameter update. This is typically done in mini-batch gradient descent, where the model processes a batch of data, computes the gradients, and then updates the parameters after processing several batches.

However, to avoid unintended accumulation of gradients between iterations, you must manually zero out the gradients after each update. PyTorch provides the `optimizer.zero_grad()` method to clear old gradients before performing the next backward pass.

Here's an example:

```Python
import torch

# Example of gradient accumulation over
multiple batches

x = torch.tensor([2.0, 3.0],
requires_grad=True)

# Simulate two forward passes

for _ in range(2):

    y = x**2 + 3*x
```

```
y.sum().backward()   # Accumulating
gradients

# Print accumulated gradients

print(x.grad)   # Gradients from both
forward passes
```

After the two backward passes, the gradients will be accumulated in x.grad. To prevent this accumulation, you can zero out the gradients before each backward pass using optimizer.zero_grad().

2.3.5 Custom Gradients

PyTorch allows you to define your own custom gradients using the Function class. This is useful when implementing custom layers, activation functions, or optimization techniques.

To define a custom operation with a custom gradient, you can subclass torch.autograd.Function and implement the forward() and backward() methods. Here's a simplified example:

```python
Python
import torch

class MyReLU(torch.autograd.Function):

    @staticmethod

    def forward(ctx, input):

        ctx.save_for_backward(input)

        return input.clamp(min=0)

    @staticmethod

    def backward(ctx, grad_output):

        input, = ctx.saved_tensors

        grad_input = grad_output.clone()

        grad_input[input < 0] = 0

        return grad_input

# Using the custom function

x = torch.tensor([-1.0, 2.0],
requires_grad=True)
```

```
relu = MyReLU.apply

y = relu(x)

y.sum().backward()

print(x.grad)
```

In this example, MyReLU defines a custom ReLU activation function with its own gradient computation. When backward() is called, it computes the gradient of the output with respect to the input and updates the .grad attribute of x.

The ability to compute gradients automatically using PyTorch's **autograd** mechanism is one of the key reasons why PyTorch is such a popular deep learning framework. By utilizing **automatic differentiation**, PyTorch handles the tedious and error-prone task of computing gradients during backpropagation. We have explored how the **chain rule** is applied to build the computational graph, compute gradients, and how you can leverage autograd to train complex models.

Understanding the underlying principles of gradient computation, such as using the `requires_grad` attribute, controlling gradient accumulation, and defining custom gradients, will give you a deeper insight into how deep learning models are trained and optimized.

2.4 Basic Neural Network Concepts

Neural networks are the backbone of modern deep learning, and understanding the basic building blocks of neural networks is crucial for building and training models effectively in PyTorch. A neural network is essentially a system of interconnected "neurons," which are organized into layers. These neurons process and transform input data to learn patterns and make predictions.

In this section, we will break down the fundamental components of neural networks, including the architecture, layers, activation functions, and how data flows through a network during the forward pass. We will also discuss the training process and how PyTorch's features are utilized to build and train neural networks efficiently.

2.4.1 Neural Network Architecture

A neural network typically consists of the following layers:

1. **Input Layer**: This layer takes in the raw input data and passes it on to the next layer. Each neuron in this layer corresponds to a feature of the input data.

2. **Hidden Layers**: These are intermediate layers where the network processes the input data and learns abstract features. There can be one or more hidden layers in a neural network, and each layer consists of multiple neurons.

3. **Output Layer**: The final layer, where the network produces its predictions. For a classification task, the output layer might consist of neurons representing different classes, while for regression, there might be a single neuron representing the predicted value.

In PyTorch, you typically define a neural network model by subclassing the `nn.Module` class, which provides an easy way to define layers and the forward pass. Let's take a look at the components that make up the architecture of a simple neural network.

2.4.2 Neural Network Layers

Neural networks are composed of layers that transform the input data. The most common types of layers in neural networks are:

1. Fully Connected (Linear) Layer

The most common layer in a neural network is the **fully connected** or **linear layer** (nn.Linear in PyTorch). Each neuron in a fully connected layer is connected to every neuron in the previous layer, and the output of each neuron is computed as a weighted sum of the inputs, followed by a bias term. The output of this layer is passed to the next layer or used for the final prediction.

The linear transformation performed by a fully connected layer can be represented mathematically as: b

$$y = W_x + b$$

Where:

- x is the input vector,

- W is the weight matrix,

- b is the bias vector,

- y is the output vector.

In PyTorch, you can define a fully connected layer using the nn.Linear module:

```python
import torch

import torch.nn as nn

# Define a simple neural network with one
fully connected layer

class SimpleNN(nn.Module):

    def __init__(self):

        super(SimpleNN, self).__init__()

        self.fc1 = nn.Linear(3, 2)   #
Input size of 3, output size of 2

    def forward(self, x):

        return self.fc1(x)

# Instantiate the model and test it with a
random input

model = SimpleNN()

input_data = torch.randn(1, 3)  # A batch
of size 1, with 3 input features

output = model(input_data)
```

```
print(output)
```

2. Activation Functions

After a linear transformation, an activation function is typically applied to introduce non-linearity into the model. Without non-linearity, the network would essentially be equivalent to a single-layer linear model, regardless of how many layers it has. Activation functions allow the network to learn complex patterns and make more accurate predictions.

Some common activation functions include:

- **ReLU (Rectified Linear Unit)**: $f(x) = max(0, x)$. ReLU is one of the most widely used activation functions due to its simplicity and effectiveness in preventing vanishing gradients.

- **Sigmoid**: $f(x) = 1 / (1 + exp(-x))$. The sigmoid function squashes its output to a range between 0 and 1, making it suitable for binary classification tasks.

- **Tanh (Hyperbolic Tangent)**: $f(x) = (\exp(x) - \exp(-x)) / (\exp(x) + \exp(-x))$. Tanh outputs values between -1 and 1, and like sigmoid, it is used to introduce non-linearity.

In PyTorch, activation functions are provided as modules in the torch.nn package, such as nn.ReLU, nn.Sigmoid, and nn.Tanh.

Example of using ReLU activation:

```Python
class SimpleNNWithReLU(nn.Module):

    def __init__(self):

        super(SimpleNNWithReLU,
self).__init__()

        self.fc1 = nn.Linear(3, 2)

        self.relu = nn.ReLU()

    def forward(self, x):

        x = self.fc1(x)

        return self.relu(x)
```

```python
model = SimpleNNWithReLU()

output = model(input_data)

print(output)
```

3. Output Layer

The output layer's structure depends on the type of task you are solving. For binary classification, a single neuron with a sigmoid activation is commonly used, while for multi-class classification, a softmax activation is applied to multiple neurons.

For a regression task, the output layer might consist of a single neuron with no activation function (or a linear activation).

Example for binary classification:

```python
Python
class BinaryClassificationNN(nn.Module):

    def __init__(self):

            super(BinaryClassificationNN,
self).__init__()
```

```python
        self.fc1 = nn.Linear(3, 5)

        self.fc2 = nn.Linear(5, 1)

        self.sigmoid = nn.Sigmoid()

    def forward(self, x):

        x = self.fc1(x)

        x = self.fc2(x)

        return self.sigmoid(x)

model = BinaryClassificationNN()

output = model(input_data)

print(output)
```

2.4.3 Training Neural Networks

Once you have a neural network model, the next step is to **train** it. Training a neural network involves passing input data through the network, calculating the loss (error), and adjusting the model parameters (weights and biases) to minimize that error.

Forward Pass

In the forward pass, input data is passed through the network's layers, and predictions are made. The forward pass computes the output of the network based on the current state of the weights and biases.

Loss Function

The loss function (also called the objective function or cost function) is used to measure how well the network's predictions match the actual labels. Common loss functions include:

- **Mean Squared Error (MSE)**: Used for regression tasks.

- **Cross-Entropy Loss**: Used for classification tasks.

In PyTorch, loss functions are available as modules in the `torch.nn` package, such as `nn.CrossEntropyLoss` and `nn.MSELoss`.

Backward Pass and Gradient Descent

Once the loss is calculated, the **backward pass** is performed to compute gradients using the **autograd** system, as discussed earlier. Afterward, an **optimizer** (such as SGD or Adam) is used to update the model's parameters by applying the gradients and reducing the loss.

```python
import torch.optim as optim

# Instantiate the model

model = BinaryClassificationNN()

# Define a loss function and an optimizer

criterion = nn.BCELoss()    # Binary
Cross-Entropy    Loss    for    binary
classification

optimizer = optim.SGD(model.parameters(),
lr=0.01)

# Example training loop

for epoch in range(100):

    optimizer.zero_grad()    # Zero the
gradients before each pass

    output = model(input_data)  # Forward
pass
```

```
    loss = criterion(output, target_data)
# Calculate the loss

    loss.backward()           # Backward
pass (compute gradients)

    optimizer.step()          # Update the
model parameters

    if (epoch+1) % 10 == 0:

        print(f'Epoch [{epoch+1}/100],
Loss: {loss.item():.4f}')
```

Model Evaluation

After training, it's important to evaluate the model's performance using validation or test data. Evaluation involves calculating the loss and accuracy (for classification) or other relevant metrics like precision, recall, and F1 score.

A neural network is a powerful model for learning complex patterns in data, and PyTorch provides an intuitive way to build and train these models. The key components of a neural network include the **input layer**, **hidden layers**, and **output layer**, along with essential elements such as **activation functions** and **loss functions**. Once you have built the network, you can train it by performing a **forward pass**, calculating the **loss**, and then updating the model's parameters using **backpropagation** and **gradient descent**.

2.5 GPU Acceleration Basics

2.5.1 Why Are GPUs Faster Than CPUs for Deep Learning?

To understand why GPUs outperform CPUs in deep learning tasks, it's important to examine their architectural differences and computational models. CPUs are designed for general-purpose computing and optimized for sequential task execution. They have a small number of powerful cores capable of handling complex calculations, making them well-suited for tasks that require high single-threaded performance, such as running operating systems and executing application logic. However, this architecture is not ideal for the highly parallelized nature of deep learning workloads.

GPUs, in contrast, are built for parallel processing and feature thousands of smaller cores that can execute many computations simultaneously. This makes them particularly effective for matrix operations, which are the foundation of deep learning. Neural networks involve performing massive matrix multiplications, tensor operations, and gradient computations, all of which benefit significantly from the parallel computing power of GPUs. By distributing computations across hundreds or thousands of cores, GPUs can process data much faster than CPUs when training deep learning models.

Another key advantage of GPUs is their specialized memory hierarchy, which is designed to optimize throughput. While CPUs rely on large caches to store frequently used data, GPUs use high-bandwidth memory (HBM) or GDDR memory, which enables rapid data access and processing. This specialized memory architecture further enhances their efficiency in deep learning applications, where large datasets and models must be processed continuously.

2.5.2 How PyTorch Leverages GPUs with CUDA

PyTorch makes it incredibly simple to take advantage of GPU acceleration using CUDA, a parallel computing

73

framework developed by NVIDIA. CUDA allows developers to execute tensor computations on NVIDIA GPUs without requiring manual optimization for parallel execution. PyTorch integrates seamlessly with CUDA, enabling automatic device selection, memory management, and tensor computations on the GPU.

The first step in utilizing a GPU in PyTorch is to check whether CUDA is available on the system. This can be done using the `torch.cuda.is_available()` function. If a compatible NVIDIA GPU is detected, PyTorch automatically enables CUDA support.

Tensors in PyTorch can be explicitly moved to the GPU by calling the `.to(device)` or `.cuda()` methods. When a tensor is allocated on the GPU, all subsequent operations performed on it will also be executed on the GPU, ensuring optimal performance. PyTorch automatically handles device transfers when performing computations between CPU and GPU tensors, but developers must ensure that all tensors involved in an operation are on the same device.

For example, to create a tensor and move it to the GPU, the following code can be used:

```python
Python
import torch

# Check if a GPU is available

device = torch.device("cuda" if
torch.cuda.is_available() else "cpu")

# Create a tensor on the CPU

tensor_cpu = torch.rand(3, 3)

# Move the tensor to the GPU

tensor_gpu = tensor_cpu.to(device)

print("Tensor on GPU:", tensor_gpu)
```

When performing deep learning model training, the model itself must also be transferred to the GPU. This ensures that both the data and the model parameters are stored and processed on the GPU, preventing unnecessary memory transfers between the CPU and GPU. The following example demonstrates how to move a neural network model to the GPU in PyTorch:

```python
Python
import torch.nn as nn
```

```python
# Define a simple neural network model

class SimpleNN(nn.Module):

    def __init__(self):

        super(SimpleNN, self).__init__()

        self.fc1 = nn.Linear(10, 5)

    def forward(self, x):

        return self.fc1(x)

# Initialize the model

model = SimpleNN()

# Move the model to the GPU

model = model.to(device)

# Create an input tensor and move it to
the GPU

input_tensor      =      torch.rand(1,
10).to(device)

# Perform a forward pass on the GPU
```

```
output = model(input_tensor)

print("Model output:", output)
```

2.5.3 Optimizing Computations with Multiple GPUs

For even greater acceleration, PyTorch supports multi-GPU training using **Data Parallelism** and **Distributed Data Parallel (DDP)**. When training deep learning models on extremely large datasets, multiple GPUs can be utilized to distribute the computational workload.

The `torch.nn.DataParallel` module provides a simple way to parallelize a model across multiple GPUs. It automatically splits the input data, processes it on multiple GPUs, and combines the results. This method is useful for increasing throughput when training on a single machine with multiple GPUs. However, for large-scale distributed training across multiple machines, PyTorch's **Distributed Data Parallel (DDP)** framework offers even better efficiency by minimizing inter-GPU communication overhead.

To use multiple GPUs for model training, the following approach can be taken:

```python
# Use DataParallel to run the model on
multiple GPUs

if torch.cuda.device_count() > 1:

                        print(f"Using
{torch.cuda.device_count()} GPUs")

    model = nn.DataParallel(model)

# Move the model to the first GPU

model.to(device)
```

For large-scale distributed training, PyTorch provides the **torch.distributed** package, which enables scalable multi-GPU training across different nodes. This is particularly useful when working with cloud computing services like AWS, Google Cloud, or Azure.

2.5.4 GPU Memory Management and Best Practices

Since deep learning models can consume large amounts of GPU memory, efficient memory management is essential when working with PyTorch. GPUs have limited memory, and improper handling of tensors can lead to **Out of Memory (OOM)** errors. PyTorch provides built-in tools to monitor GPU memory usage and optimize performance.

The `torch.cuda.memory_allocated()` and `torch.cuda.max_memory_allocated()` functions help track memory usage. Additionally, the `torch.cuda.empty_cache()` function can free unused memory and avoid fragmentation issues.

To prevent memory leaks, tensors that are no longer needed should be explicitly deleted using the `del` statement. When working with large models, gradient accumulation techniques and mixed-precision training can be used to optimize memory consumption.

For example, the following code prints the amount of memory allocated on the GPU:

```python
print(f"Memory allocated:
{torch.cuda.memory_allocated() / 1024 **
2:.2f} MB")

print(f"Max memory allocated:
{torch.cuda.max_memory_allocated() / 1024
** 2:.2f} MB")
```

Using **Mixed Precision Training** with `torch.cuda.amp` (Automatic Mixed Precision) can significantly reduce memory consumption while maintaining model accuracy. This technique leverages lower precision (FP16) for certain calculations, reducing memory footprint and improving performance.

```python
scaler = torch.cuda.amp.GradScaler()

for data, target in dataloader:

    optimizer.zero_grad()

    with torch.cuda.amp.autocast():

        output = model(data.to(device))
```

```
            loss  =  criterion(output,
target.to(device))

    scaler.scale(loss).backward()

    scaler.step(optimizer)

    scaler.update()
```

GPUs are essential for accelerating deep learning tasks due to their ability to perform massively parallel computations. Unlike CPUs, which are optimized for sequential processing, GPUs are designed to handle large-scale matrix operations efficiently, making them ideal for deep learning. PyTorch seamlessly integrates with CUDA, enabling developers to utilize GPU acceleration with minimal effort. By leveraging PyTorch's built-in functions, tensors and models can be easily transferred to the GPU, optimizing performance and reducing training time.

For even greater efficiency, PyTorch supports multi-GPU training using Data Parallelism and Distributed Data Parallel. Additionally, best practices such as GPU memory monitoring, mixed precision training, and proper tensor management help optimize performance and prevent memory issues.

By fully utilizing GPU acceleration, deep learning practitioners can train complex models on large datasets in a fraction of the time required by CPU-based computations. In the next chapter, we will explore **data handling techniques in PyTorch**, covering how to efficiently load and preprocess data for training deep learning models.

Chapter 3: Data Handling in PyTorch

Introduction

Efficient data handling is a crucial component of deep learning workflows. In PyTorch, data loading and preprocessing are streamlined using specialized tools like the `Dataset` and `DataLoader` classes. These tools enable efficient management of large-scale datasets, batch processing, parallel data loading, and real-time data augmentation. Mastering PyTorch's data handling mechanisms is essential for building scalable and high-performance deep learning models.

This chapter delves into the key aspects of data handling in PyTorch, including:

- Working with the `Dataset` and `DataLoader` classes

- Implementing custom datasets

- Data preprocessing techniques

- Performing data augmentation

- Creating efficient data pipelines

By the end of this chapter, you will have a solid understanding of how to load, preprocess, and optimize data pipelines in PyTorch, ensuring smooth model training and evaluation.

3.1 Understanding the Dataset and DataLoader Classes

3.1.1 The Dataset Class

In PyTorch, datasets are managed using the `torch.utils.data.Dataset` class. This is an abstract class that provides a blueprint for working with data efficiently. PyTorch includes several built-in dataset classes for popular datasets like MNIST, CIFAR-10, and ImageNet through the `torchvision.datasets` module.

Each dataset in PyTorch follows a standard format, with three essential methods:

- `__init__()`: Initializes the dataset, including any preprocessing or data transformations.

- `__len__()`: Returns the total number of samples in the dataset.

- `__getitem__()`: Retrieves a specific sample from the dataset based on an index.

For example, to load the MNIST dataset using PyTorch's built-in dataset:

```
Unset
import torch

from torchvision import datasets, transforms

# Define a transformation

transform = transforms.Compose([

    transforms.ToTensor(),

    transforms.Normalize((0.5,), (0.5,))

])

# Load the MNIST dataset

mnist_train = datasets.MNIST(root="./data", train=True, transform=transform, download=True)
```

```
mnist_test = datasets.MNIST(root="./data",
train=False,          transform=transform,
download=True)
```

3.1.2 The DataLoader Class

Once a dataset is defined, it must be wrapped inside a
DataLoader, which is responsible for efficiently fetching
batches of data during training. The DataLoader class
provides several important functionalities:

- **Batching**: Groups multiple samples into
  mini-batches for efficient training.

- **Shuffling**: Randomizes the order of samples to
  reduce training bias.

- **Parallel Data Loading**: Loads data asynchronously
  using multiple worker threads.

Example usage of the DataLoader class:

```
Unset
from torch.utils.data import DataLoader
```

```
# Create DataLoaders

train_loader   =   DataLoader(mnist_train,
batch_size=64,              shuffle=True,
num_workers=2)

test_loader    =   DataLoader(mnist_test,
batch_size=64,             shuffle=False,
num_workers=2)
```

Setting `shuffle=True` ensures that training samples are randomly distributed across batches, preventing overfitting. The `num_workers` parameter defines how many CPU threads to use for data loading, improving efficiency when working with large datasets.

3.2 Creating Custom Datasets

While PyTorch provides many prebuilt datasets, in real-world applications, data is often stored in CSV files, images, or other formats. PyTorch allows you to define custom datasets by subclassing `Dataset` and implementing the required methods.

For example, if you have a dataset stored as images with corresponding labels in a CSV file:

```
Unset
import os

import pandas as pd

from PIL import Image

from torch.utils.data import Dataset

class CustomImageDataset(Dataset):

    def __init__(self, csv_file, root_dir,
transform=None):

                    self.annotations   =
pd.read_csv(csv_file)

        self.root_dir = root_dir

        self.transform = transform

    def __len__(self):

        return len(self.annotations)

    def __getitem__(self, idx):
```

```
                            img_path    =
os.path.join(self.root_dir,
self.annotations.iloc[idx, 0])

                               image    =
Image.open(img_path).convert("RGB")

                            label    =
int(self.annotations.iloc[idx, 1])


        if self.transform:

            image = self.transform(image)

        return image, label
```

Once the dataset class is defined, it can be used with the DataLoader:

```
Unset
transform = transforms.Compose([

    transforms.Resize((128, 128)),

    transforms.ToTensor()
```

```
])

dataset                          =
CustomImageDataset(csv_file="labels.csv",
root_dir="images", transform=transform)

dataloader    =    DataLoader(dataset,
batch_size=32, shuffle=True)
```

3.3 Data Preprocessing Techniques

3.3.1 Normalization

Normalization helps stabilize neural network training by scaling input data to a fixed range. PyTorch's transforms.Normalize() is commonly used to normalize image datasets:

```
Unset
transforms.Normalize(mean=[0.5, 0.5, 0.5],
std=[0.5, 0.5, 0.5])
```

3.3.2 One-Hot Encoding

Categorical labels should be converted to one-hot vectors when training classification models. PyTorch provides utilities for one-hot encoding using `F.one_hot()`:

```
Unset
import torch.nn.functional as F

labels = torch.tensor([0, 1, 2])

one_hot_labels    =    F.one_hot(labels,
num_classes=3)
```

3.4 Data Augmentation

Data augmentation artificially increases the training dataset size by applying transformations such as rotation, flipping, cropping, and color jittering. This helps models generalize better and reduces overfitting.

Example of image augmentation using `torchvision.transforms`:

```
Unset
transform = transforms.Compose([
```

```
transforms.RandomHorizontalFlip(),

transforms.RandomRotation(10),

transforms.ColorJitter(brightness=0.2,
contrast=0.2),

transforms.ToTensor()

])
```

3.5. Efficient Data Pipelines

For large-scale datasets, optimizing the data pipeline ensures fast and efficient training. Strategies for optimizing data loading include:

- Increasing `num_workers` to utilize multiple CPU threads.

- Using `pin_memory=True` to speed up GPU memory transfers.

- Prefetching data using `PersistentWorkers` in PyTorch 1.10+.

Example of an optimized DataLoader:

```
Unset
dataloader        =        DataLoader(dataset,
batch_size=64,                    shuffle=True,
num_workers=4, pin_memory=True)
```

Handling data efficiently is a fundamental step in building
deep learning models. PyTorch's `Dataset` and
`DataLoader` classes provide a structured approach to
loading, preprocessing, and batching data. Custom
datasets allow for flexible integration of real-world data
formats, while preprocessing and augmentation techniques
enhance model performance. By optimizing data pipelines,
training speed and efficiency can be significantly improved,
leading to better results in deep learning applications.

Part 2: Neural Networks with PyTorch

Chapter 4: Building Neural Networks

Introduction

Building neural networks is at the core of deep learning. PyTorch provides a flexible and intuitive API for constructing, training, and deploying neural networks efficiently. At the heart of this system is the `nn.Module` class, which serves as the foundation for creating neural network architectures. Understanding how to work with layers, activation functions, loss functions, and optimizers is essential for designing and training effective models.

This chapter covers the fundamental components of neural networks, including:

- Understanding the `nn.Module` class and its importance in PyTorch.

- Implementing linear layers to construct fully connected networks.

- Utilizing activation functions to introduce non-linearity.

- Choosing appropriate loss functions for different tasks.

- Configuring optimizers and tuning learning rates.

- Building and training your first neural network from scratch.

By the end of this chapter, you will have a solid understanding of how to structure, train, and optimize a basic neural network in PyTorch.

4.1 The nn.Module Class

4.1.1 Understanding nn.Module

In PyTorch, every neural network is a subclass of `nn.Module`. This class provides a structured way to define network layers, forward passes, and manage learnable parameters efficiently. It simplifies parameter tracking and model operations, allowing seamless integration with PyTorch's autograd system.

A simple neural network class in PyTorch typically follows this structure:

```
Unset
import torch

import torch.nn as nn

class SimpleNetwork(nn.Module):

    def __init__(self):

                        super(SimpleNetwork,
self).__init__()

        self.fc1 = nn.Linear(784, 128)  #
Fully connected layer

                self.relu = nn.ReLU()    #
Activation function

        self.fc2 = nn.Linear(128, 10)   #
Output layer

    def forward(self, x):

        x = self.fc1(x)

        x = self.relu(x)

        x = self.fc2(x)

        return x
```

By subclassing nn.Module, PyTorch automatically registers the model's parameters, making it easy to track, optimize, and save them.

4.2 Linear Layers

4.2.1 Understanding Linear Layers

Linear layers, also known as fully connected or dense layers, are fundamental components in neural networks. Each linear layer performs an affine transformation:

where represents the learnable weights, is the input, and is the bias term. PyTorch provides the nn.Linear module to implement these layers efficiently.

4.2.2 Implementing a Linear Layer in PyTorch

```
Unset
linear_layer = nn.Linear(in_features=128,
out_features=64)

x = torch.randn(32, 128)   # Batch of 32
samples, each with 128 features

output = linear_layer(x)
```

```
print(output.shape)    # Expected output:
torch.Size([32, 64])
```

Linear layers are the building blocks of deep learning architectures, forming connections between neurons across layers.

4.3 Activation Functions

4.3.1 The Importance of Activation Functions

Activation functions introduce non-linearity into neural networks, allowing them to learn complex patterns. Without activation functions, a neural network would simply perform a series of linear transformations, limiting its expressive power.

4.3.2 Common Activation Functions

- **ReLU (Rectified Linear Unit)**:

- **Sigmoid**:

- **Tanh (Hyperbolic Tangent)**:

Example implementation:

```
Unset
relu = nn.ReLU()

sigmoid = nn.Sigmoid()

tanh = nn.Tanh()
```

ReLU is the most commonly used activation function due to its simplicity and effectiveness in deep networks.

4.4 Loss Functions

4.4.1 Understanding Loss Functions

Loss functions measure the difference between predicted and actual values, guiding the optimization process. The choice of loss function depends on the problem type:

- **Mean Squared Error (MSE)**: Used for regression tasks.

- **Cross-Entropy Loss**: Used for classification problems.

Example usage:

```
Unset
loss_fn = nn.CrossEntropyLoss()

predictions = torch.randn(5, 10)  # 5
samples, 10 classes

labels = torch.tensor([1, 2, 3, 4, 0])  #
True labels

loss = loss_fn(predictions, labels)

print(loss.item())
```

4.5 Optimizers and Learning Rates

4.5.1 Choosing an Optimizer

Optimizers adjust model parameters to minimize the loss.
PyTorch provides several optimizers:

- **SGD (Stochastic Gradient Descent)**: Simple and effective for many tasks.

- **Adam (Adaptive Moment Estimation)**: Efficient and widely used.

- **RMSprop**: Useful for recurrent networks.

Example:

```
Unset
optimizer                          =
torch.optim.Adam(model.parameters(),
lr=0.001)
```

4.5.2 Learning Rate Considerations

The learning rate is a crucial hyperparameter that controls the step size of updates. Choosing an optimal learning rate can significantly impact convergence.

4.6 Building Your First Neural Network

4.6.1 Constructing the Model

```
Unset
class NeuralNetwork(nn.Module):

    def __init__(self):

                    super(NeuralNetwork,
self).__init__()
```

```python
        self.fc1 = nn.Linear(784, 128)

        self.relu = nn.ReLU()

        self.fc2 = nn.Linear(128, 10)

    def forward(self, x):

        x = self.fc1(x)

        x = self.relu(x)

        x = self.fc2(x)

return x
```

4.6.2 Training the Model

```
Unset
model = NeuralNetwork()

optimizer                                    =
torch.optim.Adam(model.parameters(),
lr=0.001)

loss_fn = nn.CrossEntropyLoss()

for epoch in range(5):
```

```
for batch in train_loader:

    inputs, labels = batch

    optimizer.zero_grad()

    outputs = model(inputs)

    loss = loss_fn(outputs, labels)

    loss.backward()

    optimizer.step()
```

Understanding the fundamental components of neural networks is essential for building deep learning models in PyTorch. The nn.Module class provides a structured approach to defining models, while linear layers, activation functions, loss functions, and optimizers form the backbone of neural networks. With this knowledge, you are now equipped to construct and train your own neural networks in PyTorch. In the next chapter, we will explore training and evaluation techniques to further enhance model performance.

Chapter 5: Training and Evaluation

5.1 Training Loop Implementation

Training a neural network in PyTorch requires a structured and well-defined approach to ensure efficient learning and generalization to unseen data. The training process consists of several key steps: feeding data through the network, computing loss, adjusting the weights using optimization algorithms, and iterating through multiple epochs until the model achieves satisfactory performance. PyTorch provides an intuitive and flexible framework to implement this workflow, allowing fine-grained control over the training dynamics.

A fundamental component of deep learning training is the training loop. During each epoch, the model processes mini-batches of data, makes predictions, computes loss by comparing predictions with ground truth labels, and updates parameters using backpropagation. The typical training loop in PyTorch follows this structure:

```python
import torch

import torch.nn as nn

import torch.optim as optim

from torch.utils.data import DataLoader

def train(model, train_loader, criterion, optimizer, num_epochs):

    for epoch in range(num_epochs):

            for inputs, labels in train_loader:

            optimizer.zero_grad()

            outputs = model(inputs)

            loss = criterion(outputs, labels)

            loss.backward()

            optimizer.step()
```

```
                                 print(f"Epoch
[{epoch+1}/{num_epochs}],              Loss:
{loss.item():.4f}")
```

5.2 Validation Techniques

To ensure the model is not simply memorizing the training data, validation techniques are crucial. After each epoch, evaluating the model on a separate validation dataset helps monitor its ability to generalize. The validation process involves disabling gradient computation to save memory and improve inference speed, running the model on unseen data, and calculating performance metrics like accuracy or loss.

```
Unset
@torch.no_grad()

def      validate(model,      val_loader,
criterion):

    total_loss = 0

    correct = 0
```

```
    total = 0

    model.eval()

    for inputs, labels in val_loader:

        outputs = model(inputs)

        loss = criterion(outputs, labels)

        total_loss += loss.item()

         predicted = torch.argmax(outputs,
dim=1)

                correct += (predicted ==
labels).sum().item()

        total += labels.size(0)

    accuracy = 100 * correct / total

               print(f"Validation    Loss:
{total_loss/len(val_loader):.4f},
Accuracy: {accuracy:.2f}%")

    model.train()
```

5.3 Model Evaluation Metrics

Assessing model performance requires evaluation metrics that quantify how well the model is learning. For classification tasks, metrics like accuracy, precision, recall, and F1-score provide meaningful insights, while regression models use mean squared error or mean absolute error. The `torchmetrics` library simplifies metric computation:

```
Unset
from torchmetrics import Accuracy,
Precision, Recall

accuracy = Accuracy()

precision = Precision()

recall = Recall()

for inputs, labels in val_loader:

    outputs = model(inputs)

        predicted = torch.argmax(outputs,
dim=1)

    acc = accuracy(predicted, labels)

    prec = precision(predicted, labels)
```

```
rec = recall(predicted, labels)

        print(f"Accuracy:    {acc:.4f},
Precision: {prec:.4f}, Recall: {rec:.4f}")
```

5.4 Debugging Strategies

Debugging training issues is essential for ensuring effective learning. Common problems include overfitting, vanishing/exploding gradients, and poor convergence. Overfitting occurs when the model performs well on training data but poorly on validation data. Techniques like dropout, data augmentation, and weight decay can mitigate this.

```
Unset
nn.Dropout(p=0.5)

nn.L1Loss()
```

Vanishing or exploding gradients can arise in deep networks, particularly with improper weight initialization or activation functions. Proper initialization methods such as Xavier or He initialization and gradient clipping help manage this issue.

```
Unset
nn.init.xavier_uniform_(model.fc1.weight)

torch.nn.utils.clip_grad_norm_(model.param
eters(), max_norm=1.0)
```

5.5 Best Practices for Training

Improving training efficiency requires adopting best practices that enhance model performance and reduce training time. Data augmentation increases training data diversity, making the model more robust. PyTorch's `torchvision.transforms` module offers various augmentation techniques:

```
Unset
import        torchvision.transforms        as
transforms

transform = transforms.Compose([

    transforms.RandomHorizontalFlip(),

    transforms.RandomRotation(10),

    transforms.ToTensor()
```

```
])
```

Batch normalization stabilizes learning by normalizing activations, and careful weight initialization prevents common training problems. Monitoring loss curves and validation performance allows early detection of potential issues, facilitating dynamic hyperparameter adjustments.

5.6 Saving and Loading Models

Saving and loading models is a crucial aspect of deep learning workflows. PyTorch allows saving model state dictionaries, which store only learned parameters, or complete checkpoints that include model architecture and optimizer states.

```
Unset
# Save model state dictionary

torch.save(model.state_dict(),
'model.pth')

# Load model
```

```
model.load_state_dict(torch.load('model.pt
h'))

model.eval()
```

Saving model checkpoints ensures training progress can be resumed if interrupted and facilitates deploying trained models in production. When reloading a model, reconstructing its architecture and restoring learned weights enable further fine-tuning or inference.

The training and evaluation of deep learning models in PyTorch require a deep understanding of training loops, validation techniques, evaluation metrics, debugging strategies, and best practices. Implementing these systematically enables the development of models that not only achieve high accuracy but also generalize effectively. The ability to save and reload models enhances the practicality of PyTorch for real-world deep learning applications.

Chapter 6: Computer Vision with PyTorch

6.1 Convolutional Neural Networks

Computer vision has seen tremendous advancements with the advent of deep learning, primarily driven by Convolutional Neural Networks (CNNs). Unlike traditional fully connected networks, CNNs leverage spatial hierarchies in images, allowing them to capture features like edges, textures, and object structures efficiently. A CNN consists of multiple layers, including convolutional layers, activation functions, pooling layers, and fully connected layers, working together to extract meaningful representations from input images.

A convolutional layer applies a set of learnable filters to an input image, producing feature maps that highlight specific patterns. These filters slide across the image, computing dot products between the filter weights and the local image patches. Pooling layers, such as max pooling, reduce the spatial dimensions of feature maps while preserving important information, making the network more robust to variations in the input.

In PyTorch, CNNs can be implemented using the `torch.nn` module. A simple CNN architecture for image classification might look like this:

```
Unset
import torch

import torch.nn as nn

import torch.nn.functional as F

class SimpleCNN(nn.Module):

    def __init__(self):

        super(SimpleCNN, self).__init__()

                        self.conv1    =
nn.Conv2d(in_channels=3,  out_channels=16,
kernel_size=3, stride=1, padding=1)

                        self.pool    =
nn.MaxPool2d(kernel_size=2,     stride=2,
padding=0)

        self.conv2 = nn.Conv2d(16, 32, 3,
1, 1)
```

```python
        self.fc1 = nn.Linear(32 * 8 * 8,
    128)

        self.fc2 = nn.Linear(128, 10)

    def forward(self, x):

        x =
self.pool(F.relu(self.conv1(x)))

        x =
self.pool(F.relu(self.conv2(x)))

        x = x.view(-1, 32 * 8 * 8)

        x = F.relu(self.fc1(x))

        x = self.fc2(x)

        return x
```

6.2 Transfer Learning

Training CNNs from scratch requires substantial amounts of data and computational resources. Transfer learning addresses this challenge by leveraging pre-trained models trained on large datasets like ImageNet. Instead of training from scratch, we can use these models as feature extractors and fine-tune them for specific tasks.

PyTorch provides access to several pre-trained models through `torchvision.models`. To use a pre-trained model and fine-tune it for a new dataset, we can freeze the lower layers and train only the final layers for our specific classification task:

```
Unset
from torchvision import models

model = models.resnet18(pretrained=True)

for param in model.parameters():

    param.requires_grad = False

num_ftrs = model.fc.in_features

model.fc = nn.Linear(num_ftrs, 5)    #
Adjusting for 5 classes
```

Fine-tuning a pre-trained model significantly reduces training time while improving performance, making it an essential technique in modern computer vision.

6.3 Popular Architectures (ResNet, VGG, etc.)

Several CNN architectures have become industry standards due to their effectiveness in image recognition. ResNet (Residual Networks) introduces skip connections that help train very deep networks by addressing vanishing gradients. VGG (Visual Geometry Group) networks use sequential convolutional layers with small receptive fields, offering a straightforward yet powerful approach to feature extraction.

In PyTorch, pre-trained versions of these models are available for easy deployment. Loading and using ResNet for inference is simple:

```
Unset
model = models.resnet50(pretrained=True)

model.eval()
```

These architectures have been widely adopted in applications such as medical imaging, self-driving cars, and automated inspection systems.

6.4 Object Detection

Object detection extends image classification by not only identifying objects but also locating them within an image. Popular models such as Faster R-CNN, YOLO (You Only Look Once), and SSD (Single Shot MultiBox Detector) have revolutionized object detection with real-time performance and high accuracy.

PyTorch's `torchvision` library provides pre-trained object detection models:

```
Unset
from torchvision.models.detection import
fasterrcnn_resnet50_fpn

model                                    =
fasterrcnn_resnet50_fpn(pretrained=True)

model.eval()
```

To perform object detection, images must be preprocessed, and the model outputs bounding boxes and class probabilities. Object detection plays a crucial role in applications such as autonomous vehicles, surveillance, and medical diagnostics.

6.5 Image Segmentation

Image segmentation involves classifying each pixel in an image, distinguishing different objects and background elements. Unlike object detection, which outputs bounding boxes, segmentation generates pixel-wise masks for fine-grained analysis.

Segmentation models like U-Net and DeepLabV3+ are commonly used for applications such as medical image analysis, satellite imagery, and autonomous driving. In PyTorch, `torchvision` provides pre-trained segmentation models:

```
Unset
from torchvision.models.segmentation
import deeplabv3_resnet101

model =
deeplabv3_resnet101(pretrained=True)

model.eval()
```

Using these models, we can perform semantic segmentation by inputting an image and obtaining a per-pixel classification mask, which can be visualized using libraries such as OpenCV or Matplotlib.

6.6 Practical Computer Vision Projects

Applying computer vision techniques to real-world scenarios demonstrates the power of deep learning. Some practical projects include:

- **Facial Recognition**: Using CNNs and embedding networks like FaceNet to identify individuals in images.

- **Medical Image Analysis**: Implementing segmentation models for tumor detection in MRI scans.

- **Autonomous Driving**: Object detection for identifying pedestrians, traffic signs, and other vehicles.

- **Retail Analytics**: Using vision models for customer behavior analysis in retail stores.

Each of these applications highlights the transformative impact of computer vision and deep learning in various industries. PyTorch provides the necessary tools to implement, train, and deploy these models efficiently, making it an invaluable framework for computer vision research and development.

By mastering the concepts of convolutional neural networks, transfer learning, and advanced techniques like object detection and segmentation, we can build powerful computer vision applications that drive innovation across multiple domains. The ability to leverage pre-trained models further accelerates development, ensuring state-of-the-art performance with minimal training effort.

Part 3: Advanced Topics

Chapter 7: Natural Language Processing

7.1 Text Preprocessing for PyTorch

Natural Language Processing (NLP) begins with transforming raw text data into a structured format suitable for machine learning models. Since neural networks operate on numerical data, textual information must first be converted into a numerical representation. This transformation process involves several essential steps, including tokenization, text normalization, and numerical encoding, each of which plays a crucial role in ensuring that the input data is effectively processed by a deep learning model.

Tokenization is the first and most fundamental step in text preprocessing. It involves breaking down sentences into smaller units such as words, subwords, or characters. The granularity of tokenization depends on the nature of the task. For instance, word-level tokenization treats each word as a separate entity, while subword-based tokenization (such as Byte Pair Encoding) allows rare words to be split into smaller, frequently occurring segments, improving model performance on unseen words. Tokenization ensures that a model can understand and process textual data effectively.

Once tokenization is completed, text normalization is performed to standardize input data. This step includes converting text to lowercase to ensure uniformity, removing punctuation marks, handling contractions, and eliminating stop words when necessary. Additionally, special characters, HTML tags, and other non-essential symbols are filtered out to reduce noise. In some cases, lemmatization and stemming techniques are applied to reduce words to their base forms, helping models generalize better by treating variations of the same word as equivalent.

After normalization, words must be converted into numerical representations for processing by deep learning models. This is commonly achieved using methods such as bag-of-words, term frequency-inverse document frequency (TF-IDF), or dense vector representations like word embeddings. Bag-of-words and TF-IDF represent text as sparse vectors, capturing word frequency but ignoring word order and context. In contrast, word embeddings such as Word2Vec, GloVe, and FastText generate dense vector representations where semantically similar words are closer in vector space, allowing models to learn meaningful word relationships.

Text sequences often vary in length, posing a challenge for neural networks that require fixed-size input. To address this, padding and truncation techniques are applied to ensure uniform sequence lengths. Padding adds extra tokens to shorter sequences, while truncation shortens longer sequences to a predefined length. These operations are especially critical for recurrent neural networks (RNNs) and transformers, which process input sequences of fixed dimensions.

Once text has been tokenized, normalized, and numerically encoded, it is prepared for integration into PyTorch's dataset and dataloader pipelines. PyTorch provides `torchtext`, a specialized library for handling text preprocessing efficiently. The `torchtext.data.Field` class facilitates tokenization, numericalization, and batching, streamlining the preprocessing workflow. By leveraging PyTorch's efficient data pipeline capabilities, preprocessed text data can be seamlessly fed into deep learning models, ensuring optimal training and inference performance.

By mastering text preprocessing techniques, practitioners can significantly improve the quality and efficiency of NLP models. Properly preprocessed text not only enhances model performance but also reduces computational overhead, enabling faster and more accurate deep learning applications in various natural language processing tasks.

7.2 Word Embeddings

Traditional one-hot encoding is an early method for representing words in NLP, where each word is represented as a high-dimensional sparse vector with a single nonzero entry. However, this approach has significant limitations. It treats all words as independent entities, failing to capture relationships between them. Additionally, it results in large and memory-intensive vectors, making it computationally inefficient.

Word embeddings solve these issues by representing words as dense, lower-dimensional vectors that preserve semantic relationships. Words with similar meanings appear closer in vector space, enabling models to understand contextual similarities and syntactic relationships. These embeddings are learned through training models on vast text corpora, where words are mapped to numerical representations based on their contextual usage.

Several widely used pre-trained word embedding models exist, including Word2Vec, GloVe, and FastText. Word2Vec, developed by Google, learns embeddings using either the Continuous Bag of Words (CBOW) or Skip-Gram model. CBOW predicts a target word based on surrounding words, while Skip-Gram predicts surrounding words given a target word. GloVe, created by Stanford, constructs word vectors by factorizing a word co-occurrence matrix, capturing global statistical information about word relationships. FastText, an extension of Word2Vec by Facebook AI, enhances word representation by breaking words into subword n-grams, improving handling of rare words and morphological variations.

In PyTorch, word embeddings can be implemented using the `torch.nn.Embedding` layer, which creates trainable embeddings that can be optimized during model training. This layer takes a vocabulary size and embedding dimension as input, producing dense vector representations for each word in the vocabulary. Additionally, pre-trained embeddings from models like Word2Vec or GloVe can be loaded into the `Embedding` layer, allowing for transfer learning. By setting `requires_grad=False`, these embeddings can be used as fixed representations, or they can be fine-tuned on domain-specific data.

The advantage of word embeddings is their ability to capture nuanced semantic and syntactic relationships.

They allow NLP models to generalize better by understanding word context rather than relying solely on exact word matches. This is particularly useful in tasks such as sentiment analysis, text classification, machine translation, and question answering. By leveraging high-quality word embeddings, PyTorch-based NLP models achieve improved accuracy and efficiency, leading to more robust and context-aware language processing systems.

7.3 RNNs and LSTMs

Recurrent Neural Networks (RNNs) and Long Short-Term Memory (LSTM) networks are both types of neural networks specifically designed to deal with sequential data. These types of data can be found in a variety of real-world applications, such as time series forecasting, language modeling, and speech recognition. The primary strength of RNNs is their ability to maintain hidden states, which allows them to retain memory from previous time steps. This feature enables RNNs to process sequences where the order of data is essential, such as text or audio, and learn dependencies across time.

7.3.1 Recurrent Neural Networks (RNNs)

RNNs are designed with loops that connect neurons to each other, enabling them to pass information from one step of the sequence to the next. The network processes the input sequentially, generating outputs and updating its hidden state at each step based on the current input and the previous hidden state. The hidden state, which is a vector, serves as the network's memory, encoding information from prior time steps.

However, standard RNNs face a significant challenge known as the **vanishing gradient problem**. This issue arises during the backpropagation step of training, where gradients (used to update the weights of the network) can become very small as they are propagated backward through many time steps. This can make it difficult for the network to learn long-term dependencies, as the influence of earlier time steps effectively "vanishes" over time. In simple terms, when an RNN is trained on long sequences, the model struggles to remember information from earlier in the sequence because the gradients are too small to effectively update the weights.

7.3.2 Long Short-Term Memory Networks (LSTMs)

LSTM networks were specifically developed to address the vanishing gradient problem that limits RNNs. LSTMs maintain the concept of hidden states but incorporate **gating mechanisms** to better control the flow of information. These gates regulate what information should be retained in memory, and what should be discarded, making them more effective at capturing long-range dependencies in sequences.

An LSTM consists of three key components:

1. **Input Gate**: This gate controls how much of the new information generated at each time step should be added to the cell state (the memory). It uses the current input and the previous hidden state to decide what new information should be stored in memory.

2. **Forget Gate**: The forget gate is responsible for deciding what portion of the existing memory should be discarded. In each time step, the model can forget some part of the previous memory based on the current input and hidden state, allowing it to focus on more relevant information.

3. **Output Gate**: The output gate determines what part of the cell state will be outputted as the hidden state for the current time step. The hidden state, which is passed to the next time step, will be influenced by both the previous hidden state and the updated memory.

Together, these gates allow LSTMs to regulate the flow of information and keep track of long-term dependencies in a way that traditional RNNs cannot. This makes LSTMs particularly useful in tasks where the network needs to "remember" information for long periods of time, such as language modeling or machine translation.

In practice, LSTM layers are implemented in frameworks like **PyTorch** using `nn.LSTM`. The `nn.LSTM` module processes sequences in a recursive manner, passing data through the network and updating the hidden states at each time step. It requires input sequences in the form of tensors, where each input corresponds to a time step in the sequence. The LSTM module returns two key components: the output sequence (which contains the hidden state for each time step) and the final hidden and cell states (which can be used for future time steps in the sequence).

7.3.3 Bidirectional LSTMs

While standard LSTMs process sequences in a unidirectional manner (from the beginning of the sequence to the end), **bidirectional LSTMs** (BiLSTMs) offer a performance boost by processing the sequence in both forward and backward directions. This dual-pass approach allows the network to capture dependencies from both the past and the future in a given sequence. For example, in natural language processing (NLP) tasks, understanding the context from both the previous and the following words can lead to better model performance. By processing the sequence in both directions, BiLSTMs can capture richer context and more nuanced relationships between words.

In PyTorch, the bidirectional functionality can be enabled by setting the `bidirectional=True` parameter when creating the `nn.LSTM` layer. This creates two separate hidden states, one for the forward pass and another for the backward pass, and then combines them.

7.3.4 Applications of LSTMs

LSTMs are widely used across various domains, particularly in fields that require sequential data processing. Some common applications include:

- **Sentiment Analysis**: LSTMs are highly effective in analyzing text data, such as movie reviews or social media posts, to determine the sentiment (positive, negative, neutral) of the text. The ability to capture long-term dependencies allows LSTMs to understand contextual nuances that may influence sentiment.

- **Machine Translation**: LSTMs are employed in sequence-to-sequence models for machine translation. They help map sequences from one language (e.g., English) to another language (e.g., French) while considering both the past and future context of each word in the sequence.

- **Speech Recognition**: LSTMs are frequently used in speech-to-text models, where they convert audio signals into textual representations. By capturing the temporal dependencies in audio sequences, LSTMs improve the model's ability to recognize words based on their context in the sentence.

LSTMs offer a powerful solution to the challenges faced by traditional RNNs, particularly in the context of learning long-term dependencies in sequential data. By using gating mechanisms to control the flow of information, LSTMs are better suited for tasks such as natural language processing, time series forecasting, and speech recognition. Bidirectional LSTMs further enhance the ability of the model to understand both past and future context, leading to improved performance on a wide range of sequential tasks.

7.4 Transformer Architecture

The **Transformer architecture** has revolutionized the field of Natural Language Processing (NLP) by introducing a new way of handling sequential data that does not rely on the recurrent structures used in traditional models like RNNs or LSTMs. Instead of processing input sequences step by step, transformers leverage a powerful mechanism called **self-attention**, which allows the model to analyze the relationships between all words in a sequence simultaneously, regardless of their position relative to each other. This ability to handle dependencies between words without relying on their sequential order allows transformers to process input data in parallel, significantly improving computational efficiency and enabling large-scale models like GPT and BERT.

7.4.1 Self-Attention Mechanism

At the core of the transformer model lies the **self-attention mechanism**, which enables the model to weigh the importance of each word in a sequence relative to all the other words, irrespective of their distance in the input sequence. This mechanism is often referred to as **scaled dot-product attention**, and it works by calculating three key vectors for each word in the sequence:

1. **Query (Q)**: Represents the current word that is seeking information.

2. **Key (K)**: Represents each word in the sequence as a key, which will be compared against the query.

3. **Value (V)**: Represents the actual information associated with each word.

The self-attention process computes an attention score for each pair of words in the sequence. The attention score is determined by calculating the dot product between the query and the key vectors, then scaling the result to prevent the values from growing too large. These scores are passed through a softmax function to normalize them, which ensures that the attention scores sum to one. The final output is a weighted sum of the values, where the weights are determined by the attention scores. This process allows the model to focus on different parts of the sequence for each word, effectively "attending" to relevant words regardless of their position in the sequence.

The self-attention mechanism is powerful because it allows the transformer model to capture **long-range dependencies** between words that may be far apart in the sequence, something that RNNs and LSTMs struggle with due to their sequential nature. Since transformers process the entire sequence at once, they can also take advantage of **parallelization**, making them significantly more efficient when handling large datasets.

7.4.2 Transformer Layers: Encoder-Decoder Architecture

A transformer consists of multiple layers of self-attention and feedforward networks. The typical transformer architecture is divided into two parts: the **encoder** and the **decoder**. Each part consists of several identical layers stacked on top of each other.

- **Encoder**: The encoder's job is to process the input sequence and produce an output representation. Each encoder layer has two main components: the self-attention mechanism and a feedforward neural network. The self-attention mechanism processes the input sequence and computes the attention scores, while the feedforward network applies transformations to the data to capture more complex relationships. Each layer in the encoder

137

also includes residual connections and layer normalization to stabilize training.

- **Decoder**: The decoder takes the encoder's output and uses it to generate the final output sequence. Like the encoder, the decoder contains self-attention layers and feedforward networks. However, in addition to the self-attention mechanism, the decoder has a **cross-attention** layer that allows it to focus on specific parts of the encoder's output. This helps the decoder generate outputs that are closely related to the context provided by the encoder, especially useful in tasks like machine translation.

The encoder and decoder work together in parallel to produce a sequence-to-sequence transformation. The key benefit of this architecture is its ability to handle long-range dependencies and relationships in data, as well as its efficiency in processing large sequences due to parallelization.

7.4.3 Positional Encoding

Since transformers process the entire sequence at once, they do not inherently retain information about the order of words in the sequence (unlike RNNs or LSTMs). To solve this problem, transformers introduce **positional**

encodings. These encodings are added to the input embeddings of the words to provide the model with information about the positions of words in the sequence.

Positional encodings are typically generated using sinusoidal functions, where each dimension of the positional encoding corresponds to a different frequency. This ensures that the model can differentiate between words based on their relative positions in the sequence. By adding positional encoding to the word embeddings, the transformer model can retain the sequence order and capture the structural dependencies between words.

7.4.4 Efficiency and Scalability

Transformers have been widely recognized for their efficiency in large-scale NLP tasks, especially when compared to traditional models like RNNs or LSTMs. One of the main reasons for this efficiency is that transformers do not rely on sequential processing. In an RNN, each word must be processed in order, one step at a time, which limits parallelism and increases computation time. In contrast, the self-attention mechanism in transformers allows for **parallelization**, where all words can be processed simultaneously. This makes transformers particularly well-suited for training on large datasets and for scaling up to massive models.

Another advantage is that transformers can capture complex relationships between all words in a sequence, regardless of their distance, without being hindered by the vanishing gradient problem that affects RNNs. As a result, transformers have achieved state-of-the-art performance in a wide range of NLP tasks, such as machine translation, text generation, and question answering.

7.4.5   PyTorch   Implementation: `torch.nn.Transformer`

In PyTorch, the `torch.nn.Transformer` module provides an easy-to-use implementation of the transformer architecture. This module abstracts away the complexities of building a transformer from scratch and provides efficient implementations of key components like the self-attention mechanism, feedforward networks, and positional encoding.

The `torch.nn.Transformer` module is designed to handle both the encoder and decoder parts of the transformer, and it provides flexibility in defining the number of layers, the size of the model, and other parameters like the number of attention heads. The attention mechanism within the transformer is implemented by computing the **query**, **key**, and **value** matrices at each layer, and the output is generated by applying these attention scores to the values. The module also supports multi-head attention, where multiple attention mechanisms run in parallel, allowing the model to focus on different parts of the sequence at the same time.

Applications of Transformers

Transformers have become the foundation for many state-of-the-art models in NLP, including:

- **BERT (Bidirectional Encoder Representations from Transformers)**: A transformer-based model that is pre-trained on vast amounts of text data and fine-tuned for specific tasks like text classification or named entity recognition.

- **GPT (Generative Pretrained Transformer)**: A language model that uses transformers for text generation, capable of producing coherent and contextually appropriate text across a wide range of domains.

- **T5 (Text-to-Text Transfer Transformer)**: A model that treats every NLP task as a text-to-text problem, enabling the same model architecture to handle tasks like translation, summarization, and question answering.

The transformer architecture has reshaped the way NLP tasks are approached by replacing the sequential nature of RNNs with the self-attention mechanism, which allows for greater parallelization and better handling of long-range dependencies. The use of positional encodings ensures that word order is preserved, and the overall design makes transformers highly efficient for large-scale NLP tasks. With frameworks like PyTorch providing simplified implementations, transformers have become the go-to architecture for a wide variety of NLP applications.

7.5 BERT and Modern Language Models

BERT (Bidirectional Encoder Representations from Transformers) has fundamentally changed the landscape of Natural Language Processing (NLP) by introducing a powerful pre-training strategy for transformer-based models. Before BERT, most NLP models processed text in a **left-to-right** manner, where the context from preceding words was used to predict the next word in a sequence. This approach, while effective, often missed crucial information from the **right context** (i.e., the words that follow), which can be vital for understanding the meaning of a word in a given sentence.

BERT, on the other hand, uses a **bidirectional approach**, which means that it takes both the left and right contexts into account when learning word representations. This is achieved by using a **transformer architecture** that processes the entire sequence simultaneously, rather than sequentially. As a result, BERT captures more comprehensive, context-dependent word representations, which significantly improves the model's ability to understand language nuances, resolve ambiguity, and handle long-range dependencies in text.

7.5.1 BERT's Pre-training and Fine-tuning Process

BERT undergoes a two-stage training process: **pre-training** and **fine-tuning**. These stages allow the model to first learn general language representations from large amounts of text data and then specialize these representations for specific NLP tasks.

1. Pre-training

During the pre-training phase, BERT learns to predict words and their relationships in a generic, unsupervised manner. The pre-training involves two main tasks:

- **Masked Language Modeling (MLM)**: In this task, some percentage of the words in the input sequence are randomly replaced with a special [MASK] token. BERT's job is to predict the original value of the masked words based on their surrounding context. This task allows BERT to learn the relationship between words by considering the entire sentence, both the left and right context, which is essential for learning deep contextualized word embeddings.

- **Next Sentence Prediction (NSP)**: In this task, BERT is provided with pairs of sentences, and the model must predict whether the second sentence logically follows the first one. This task is particularly useful for applications that require sentence-level understanding, such as question answering and natural language inference. By learning the relationships between sentences, BERT is able to improve its understanding of discourse and sentence structure.

Through these pre-training tasks, BERT learns general language features that can be transferred to various downstream tasks. The pre-trained model is capable of capturing semantic relationships, syntactic structures, and contextual word meanings, making it a versatile foundation for many NLP applications.

2. Fine-tuning

After the pre-training stage, BERT undergoes **fine-tuning**, where it is adapted to perform specific NLP tasks such as text classification, named entity recognition (NER), or question answering. Fine-tuning involves training the model on a smaller, labeled dataset related to the target task. Importantly, during fine-tuning, all of BERT's parameters are updated, allowing the model to specialize its learned representations for the task at hand.

Fine-tuning is efficient because it leverages the knowledge BERT has already acquired during pre-training, requiring relatively less task-specific data to achieve high performance. For instance, in the case of text classification, BERT can be fine-tuned to classify a text sample as positive or negative by adding a task-specific classification layer on top of the pre-trained model. Similarly, in question answering, BERT can be fine-tuned to predict the start and end positions of an answer within a given passage of text.

7.5.2 Pre-trained BERT Models and Integration with PyTorch

One of the key innovations introduced by BERT is the availability of **pre-trained models**. These models are trained on large, diverse text corpora (such as the entire Wikipedia and books corpus) and can be downloaded and fine-tuned for specific tasks. The availability of pre-trained models makes it easy to leverage BERT's powerful representations without needing to train a model from scratch.

The **transformers library** by Hugging Face is one of the most popular tools for working with pre-trained BERT models. This library provides a simple interface to download, fine-tune, and deploy models like BERT, integrating seamlessly with frameworks like **PyTorch**. The transformers library also supports many other popular models like GPT, T5, and RoBERTa, which are built on the same transformer architecture.

By using pre-trained models from the transformers library, practitioners can focus on task-specific customization rather than spending time and resources on training large models from the ground up. These pre-trained models can be applied to a wide range of NLP tasks, such as **sentiment analysis**, **named entity recognition (NER)**, **text summarization**, and more.

7.5.3 GPT (Generative Pre-trained Transformer)

In addition to BERT, **GPT (Generative Pre-trained Transformer)** is another highly influential language model that has gained significant attention, especially for text generation tasks. While BERT is focused on learning bidirectional word representations for understanding tasks, GPT is designed with an emphasis on generating coherent text by predicting the next word in a sequence. This difference stems from the fact that BERT uses a masked language modeling approach (predicting masked words in context), while GPT uses a **left-to-right causal language modeling** approach, where the model predicts the next word based on the words that come before it.

GPT models are particularly effective for **text generation**, **chatbot development**, and **dialogue systems**, as they excel at producing fluent, contextually appropriate text. GPT's architecture is a decoder-only transformer, where each word is generated sequentially, conditioning on the preceding words. This makes GPT ideal for applications where generating human-like text is crucial, such as story generation, code synthesis, or conversational agents.

Like BERT, GPT models are pre-trained on massive corpora and can be fine-tuned for specific tasks. GPT-3, one of the largest and most advanced versions of GPT, has demonstrated remarkable capabilities in text generation, completing sentences, answering questions, and even generating creative content like poetry and essays.

7.6 Text Classification and Generation

Text classification and **text generation** are two foundational tasks in Natural Language Processing (NLP), each with distinct goals and applications. While text classification involves categorizing a text into predefined categories, text generation focuses on producing coherent and contextually appropriate text based on an input prompt. Both tasks are pivotal in a variety of real-world scenarios, and advances in deep learning have significantly improved performance in both areas, especially with the advent of transformer-based models.

7.6.1 Text Classification

Text classification is the task of assigning predefined labels or categories to text data based on its content. This task is widely used in applications such as **sentiment analysis** (determining whether a text expresses positive or negative sentiment), **spam detection** (identifying whether an email is spam or not), and **topic categorization** (classifying articles into categories like sports, politics, or technology). The primary goal is to build a model that can automatically predict the label of a given piece of text, helping automate tasks that would otherwise require manual intervention.

A basic **text classification model** typically consists of the following components:

1. **Embedding Layer**: This layer is responsible for converting words or tokens into vector representations. Words in the input text are mapped to dense vectors, capturing semantic information about each word. Common embedding techniques include Word2Vec, GloVe, and more recently, **transformer-based embeddings** such as those from models like BERT.

2. **Recurrent or Transformer Layers**: After the embedding layer, the model processes the input sequence using either **LSTM (Long Short-Term Memory)** units or **transformer layers**. LSTMs are a type of recurrent neural network (RNN) capable of handling sequences with long-term dependencies, while transformers leverage self-attention mechanisms to capture relationships

149

between words regardless of their distance in the sequence. Transformer-based models, such as BERT or RoBERTa, are often preferred due to their superior performance in handling complex relationships and long-range dependencies in text.

3. **Fully Connected Layer**: After the sequence is processed by the LSTM or transformer layers, the model typically includes a fully connected (dense) layer, which outputs the predicted class label. The final prediction is made using a **softmax activation function**, which assigns a probability to each class label, allowing the model to select the most likely category.

One of the most significant advances in text classification has been the **fine-tuning of pre-trained models** such as BERT. Fine-tuning involves adjusting a pre-trained model, which has already learned general language representations from a large corpus, on a specific classification task. This approach significantly improves accuracy, especially when the available labeled data for a specific task is limited. Fine-tuned models benefit from the ability to leverage knowledge about syntax, semantics, and context that the pre-trained model has learned, leading to improved performance on tasks such as sentiment analysis, NER (named entity recognition), and more.

By using pre-trained transformer models and fine-tuning them for specific tasks, it is possible to achieve state-of-the-art results in text classification tasks with relatively little task-specific data.

7.6.2 Text Generation

Text generation is the process of producing coherent and contextually relevant text from an initial input or prompt. This task has seen remarkable progress in recent years with the development of large, pre-trained language models like **GPT (Generative Pre-trained Transformer)**. These models are capable of generating human-like text by learning the structure, grammar, and meaning of language from massive amounts of text data. Text generation is used in a wide range of applications, from **story generation** and **content creation** to **chatbots** and **dialogue systems**.

The process of text generation in models like GPT is typically based on a **causal (unidirectional) language model**, where the model predicts the next word in the sequence given the previous words. The model is trained to generate text one word at a time, conditioning on the words that have been generated so far. As a result, GPT models excel at producing long-form, coherent text based on the initial input, whether it's completing a sentence, generating a paragraph, or creating an entire article.

Text generation is an essential part of many NLP applications, including:

- **Chatbot Development**: By generating responses to user inputs, language models can power intelligent conversational agents capable of holding contextually appropriate conversations with users. The goal is to produce responses that not only make sense but also feel natural and coherent within the context of the conversation.

- **Content Creation and Text Synthesis**: Models like GPT-3 are capable of generating creative text, such as writing essays, stories, poems, or even code. These models are trained on diverse datasets, allowing them to produce a wide range of outputs across various domains.

- **Machine Translation**: In translation tasks, sequence-to-sequence models based on encoder-decoder architectures are used to translate text from one language to another. These models typically use an encoder to process the input text in the source language and a decoder to generate the translated text in the target language.

Sequence-to-sequence models are particularly important for tasks that require transforming one sequence of text into another, such as machine translation, summarization, and dialogue systems. These models use an **encoder-decoder architecture**, where the encoder processes the input sequence and encodes it into a fixed-length vector (or a sequence of vectors), and the decoder generates the output sequence based on this encoded information. The attention mechanism, particularly the **self-attention** mechanism in transformers, plays a key role in improving the performance of these models by allowing the model to focus on different parts of the input sequence when generating the output.

7.6.3 PyTorch for Text Classification and Generation

By mastering these **text classification** and **text generation** techniques, PyTorch users can build highly sophisticated models capable of handling a wide range of language tasks. PyTorch provides a variety of tools and libraries, such as **torchtext** for preprocessing and tokenization, and **transformers** for using pre-trained models, that make it easier to implement cutting-edge solutions for NLP tasks.

The key concepts to understand in building robust NLP models include:

- **Embeddings**: Word embeddings are essential for capturing the semantic meaning of words. Pre-trained embeddings, such as those from Word2Vec, GloVe, or BERT, can be used to initialize the model's word representations.

- **Sequence Models**: Models like **RNNs**, **LSTMs**, and **transformers** are the backbone of NLP applications. Sequence models help process input text and capture relationships between words over time (RNNs, LSTMs) or across the entire sequence (transformers).

- **Transformers**: Transformers have become the go-to architecture for NLP tasks due to their ability to handle long-range dependencies and perform parallel processing of sequences. Pre-trained transformer models such as BERT and GPT can be fine-tuned for specific tasks to achieve state-of-the-art results.

By understanding these key components, developers and researchers can build powerful NLP systems that can tackle real-world challenges such as sentiment analysis, machine translation, content generation, and more. The flexibility and performance of modern models make them highly applicable in a wide range of industries, from customer service and healthcare to entertainment and education.

Chapter 8: Advanced Model Architectures

In this chapter, we will explore some of the most advanced and powerful model architectures in deep learning, each of which serves a unique purpose and can be adapted to solve various complex tasks. These architectures are often at the cutting edge of AI research and have broad applications in fields such as computer vision, natural language processing, generative modeling, and even bioinformatics.

8.1 GANs (Generative Adversarial Networks) Implementation

Generative Adversarial Networks (GANs), introduced by Ian Goodfellow in 2014, represent one of the most exciting advancements in the field of machine learning, particularly in the realm of **generative modeling**. A GAN consists of two neural networks: a **generator** and a **discriminator**. These networks are trained together in a game-theoretic setup where the generator aims to produce realistic data (images, text, etc.), while the discriminator tries to distinguish between real data (from the training set) and fake data (produced by the generator).

- **Generator Network**: The generator takes random noise as input and generates data that mimics the distribution of the real data. The goal of the generator is to improve over time so that its generated data is indistinguishable from real data.

- **Discriminator Network**: The discriminator takes real and fake data as input and outputs a probability of whether the input is real or fake. Its task is to become better at detecting the fake data generated by the generator.

The training process involves the generator improving its ability to deceive the discriminator, while the discriminator becomes better at identifying fake data. This **adversarial** training process continues until the generator creates data that is indistinguishable from real data, and the discriminator reaches its maximum capacity for distinguishing real from fake.

Applications of GANs:

- **Image Generation**: GANs can generate highly realistic images from random noise, as seen in applications like **Deepfakes** or **artificial image synthesis** (such as generating human faces or landscapes).

157

- **Data Augmentation**: GANs can generate synthetic data to augment training datasets, especially in scenarios where labeled data is scarce.

- **Style Transfer**: GANs can be used for tasks like transferring the style of one image (e.g., a painting) to another image (e.g., a photograph).

Implementing GANs in PyTorch: GANs are implemented by defining both the generator and discriminator networks, which are typically **fully connected** or **convolutional neural networks** (CNNs), and training them with a combination of **binary cross-entropy** loss and optimizers like **Adam**.

```python
Python
import torch

import torch.nn as nn

import torch.optim as optim

# Generator model

class Generator(nn.Module):

    def __init__(self, z_dim):
```

```python
        super(Generator, self).__init__()

        self.fc = nn.Sequential(

            nn.Linear(z_dim, 256),

            nn.ReLU(),

            nn.Linear(256, 512),

            nn.ReLU(),

            nn.Linear(512, 1024),

            nn.ReLU(),

            nn.Linear(1024, 28*28),   #
Example for MNIST

            nn.Tanh()

        )

    def forward(self, z):

        return self.fc(z).view(-1, 1, 28,
28)

# Discriminator model
```

```python
class Discriminator(nn.Module):

    def __init__(self):

                super(Discriminator,
self).__init__()

        self.fc = nn.Sequential(

        nn.Linear(28*28, 1024),

        nn.LeakyReLU(0.2),

        nn.Linear(1024, 512),

        nn.LeakyReLU(0.2),

        nn.Linear(512, 256),

        nn.LeakyReLU(0.2),

        nn.Linear(256, 1),

        nn.Sigmoid()

        )

    def forward(self, x):

        return self.fc(x.view(-1, 28*28))
```

```python
# Initialize models and optimizers

z_dim = 100

generator = Generator(z_dim)

discriminator = Discriminator()

optimizer_g =
optim.Adam(generator.parameters(),
lr=0.0002, betas=(0.5, 0.999))

optimizer_d =
optim.Adam(discriminator.parameters(),
lr=0.0002, betas=(0.5, 0.999))

# Loss function

criterion = nn.BCELoss()
```

8.2 Autoencoders

An **Autoencoder** is a type of neural network used for **unsupervised learning**. It learns to compress (encode) input data into a lower-dimensional latent space and then reconstructs the original input from this compressed representation. Autoencoders are typically composed of two parts:

- **Encoder**: The encoder network maps the input data to a lower-dimensional latent space. The output of the encoder is a compressed representation of the input data.

- **Decoder**: The decoder network takes the compressed latent representation and reconstructs it back to the original input format. The network is trained to minimize the reconstruction error, such as Mean Squared Error (MSE), between the original and the reconstructed data.

Applications:

- **Dimensionality Reduction**: Autoencoders can be used to reduce the number of features in a dataset, similar to Principal Component Analysis (PCA), but in a more flexible, nonlinear way.

- **Anomaly Detection**: By training an autoencoder on normal data, it can be used to detect anomalies based on reconstruction error. If the autoencoder fails to reconstruct the input accurately, it may indicate an outlier or anomaly.

- **Denoising**: Denoising autoencoders are trained to remove noise from corrupted inputs, making them useful in signal processing and image processing.

Implementing Autoencoders in PyTorch: Here is a simple implementation of an autoencoder for image data:

```python
Python
class Autoencoder(nn.Module):

    def __init__(self):

                super(Autoencoder,
self).__init__()

        self.encoder = nn.Sequential(

                    nn.Conv2d(1,   32,
kernel_size=3, stride=2, padding=1),

            nn.ReLU(),

                    nn.Conv2d(32,  64,
kernel_size=3, stride=2, padding=1),

            nn.ReLU()

        )

        self.decoder = nn.Sequential(
```

```python
            nn.ConvTranspose2d(64, 32,
    kernel_size=3, stride=2, padding=1),

            nn.ReLU(),

            nn.ConvTranspose2d(32, 1,
    kernel_size=3, stride=2, padding=1),

            nn.Sigmoid()

        )

    def forward(self, x):

        x = self.encoder(x)

        x = self.decoder(x)

        return x

autoencoder = Autoencoder()
```

8.3 Siamese Networks

A **Siamese network** is a type of neural network architecture that consists of two or more identical sub-networks, which share the same weights and parameters. Siamese networks are primarily used for

metric learning tasks, where the goal is to learn a similarity function between input pairs. These networks are often applied in tasks like **face verification**, **signature verification**, and **one-shot learning**.

The two networks take two different inputs and output embeddings (vector representations) for each input. The embeddings are then compared, typically using a distance metric such as **Euclidean distance** or **cosine similarity**. The network is trained to minimize the distance between similar inputs and maximize the distance between dissimilar inputs.

Applications:

- **Face Verification**: Siamese networks can be used to verify whether two face images belong to the same person.

- **One-shot Learning**: Siamese networks enable models to recognize objects or faces from just one example, making them valuable in situations where labeled data is scarce.

Implementing Siamese Networks in PyTorch: Here is a basic implementation of a Siamese network:

Python

```python
class SiameseNetwork(nn.Module):

    def __init__(self):

        super(SiameseNetwork,
self).__init__()

        self.convnet = nn.Sequential(

            nn.Conv2d(1,  64,
kernel_size=3),

            nn.ReLU(),

            nn.Conv2d(64,  128,
kernel_size=3),

            nn.ReLU(),

            nn.Flatten()

        )

    def forward_one(self, x):

        return self.convnet(x)

    def forward(self, input1, input2):

        output1 = self.forward_one(input1)
```

```
output2 = self.forward_one(input2)

return output1, output2
```

8.4 Attention Mechanisms

Attention mechanisms allow models to focus on specific parts of the input when making predictions, instead of treating all parts equally. This idea is especially prominent in **transformer models** used in NLP tasks such as **machine translation** and **text summarization**. The **self-attention mechanism** computes a weighted sum of all input tokens based on their relevance to each other, helping the model capture long-range dependencies and contextual relationships in the input sequence.

Applications:

- **Machine Translation**: Attention mechanisms help models focus on relevant parts of the input sequence when translating text, leading to better translations.

- **Text Summarization**: In tasks like summarization, attention mechanisms allow models to focus on important parts of the document to generate coherent summaries.

8.5 Graph Neural Networks (GNNs)

Graph Neural Networks (GNNs) are a class of neural networks designed to work directly with **graph-structured data**. In GNNs, each node in the graph aggregates information from its neighboring nodes to learn node and graph representations. This architecture is widely used in tasks like **social network analysis**, **recommendation systems**, and **drug discovery**.

Applications:

- **Social Network Analysis**: GNNs can be used to predict links (relationships between users) or classify nodes (e.g., user profiles).

- **Recommendation Systems**: GNNs can model user-item interactions and predict user preferences.

8.6 Custom Architecture Design

Designing **custom neural network architectures** is essential when off-the-shelf models cannot fully address a particular problem. PyTorch allows users to build custom architectures from scratch by defining individual layers and the forward pass. Custom architectures enable more flexibility and control, allowing researchers and engineers to experiment with novel approaches for specific tasks.

Custom architectures can integrate various components, such as:

- **Hybrid models** that combine CNNs for image processing with RNNs for sequential data.

- **Ensemble models** that combine multiple models to improve performance.

Chapter 9: Model Optimization

Optimizing deep learning models is essential for deploying them efficiently in real-world applications. This involves making models smaller, faster, and more memory-efficient without significantly compromising their accuracy. This chapter delves into several key techniques for model optimization, including model quantization, pruning, knowledge distillation, distributed training, performance optimization, and memory management.

9.1 Model Quantization

Model quantization is a technique used to reduce the precision of numerical computations in a deep learning model. Instead of using 32-bit floating-point numbers (FP32), models are often quantized to 16-bit floating-point numbers (FP16) or even 8-bit integers (INT8). This reduction in precision leads to smaller model sizes, faster computation, and lower memory requirements, which is particularly useful when deploying models on devices with limited resources, such as mobile phones or embedded systems.

There are different types of quantization. One approach is **post-training quantization**, where a trained model is converted to lower precision after the training phase. During this process, calibration data is used to minimize any potential loss in accuracy due to the reduced precision. Another approach is **quantization-aware training (QAT)**, where the model is trained with quantization in mind, simulating lower precision during training and allowing the model to adapt to the lower-precision computations before deployment.

Quantization can dramatically reduce the model size and improve inference speed, especially when deployed on specialized hardware like GPUs, TPUs, or mobile processors that support low-precision operations. However, there is typically a trade-off between accuracy and performance, so it's important to carefully evaluate the effects of quantization on the model's output.

Code Example: Model Quantization in PyTorch

```python
import torch

import torch.quantization
```

```python
# Load a pre-trained model (e.g.,
ResNet18)

model                              =
torchvision.models.resnet18(pretrained=Tru
e)

# Prepare the model for quantization

model.eval()     # Set the model to
evaluation mode

model = torch.quantization.prepare(model,
inplace=False)

# Calibrate the model using example data

# Here, we simply pass the model an
example input

example_input = torch.randn(1, 3, 224,
224)  # Example image

model(example_input)

# Convert the model to its quantized
version
```

```
quantized_model                              =
torch.quantization.convert(model,
inplace=False)

# Check the type of the quantized model

print(quantized_model)
```

9.2 Pruning Techniques

Pruning involves reducing the size of a deep learning model by removing unnecessary weights or neurons. This helps in reducing the model's computational complexity and memory usage, making it more efficient without significant losses in performance.

Pruning can be applied to both **weights** and **neural network layers**. In weight pruning, individual weights with small magnitudes, which contribute little to the model's decision-making process, are removed. This results in a sparse network, where many of the connections are zero, thus saving memory and speeding up inference. **Structured pruning** can be applied to entire neurons, filters, or layers, removing entire components of the model that are not contributing significantly to performance.

The challenge in pruning is maintaining model accuracy after removing parts of the network. Often, pruning is followed by **fine-tuning**, where the model is retrained on the same data to recover any accuracy lost during the pruning process.

Pruning is particularly valuable for deploying deep learning models on edge devices where memory and compute resources are constrained. By reducing the number of parameters, pruning can make models more manageable and responsive, improving their ability to run efficiently in production environments.

Code Example: Pruning in PyTorch

```python
Python
import torch

import torch.nn as nn

import torch.nn.utils.prune as prune

# Create a simple model with a Linear
layer

class SimpleModel(nn.Module):

    def __init__(self):
```

```python
                    super(SimpleModel,
self).__init__()

        self.fc = nn.Linear(10, 10)

    def forward(self, x):

        return self.fc(x)

# Create an instance of the model

model = SimpleModel()

# Apply pruning on the linear layer

prune.random_unstructured(model.fc,
name="weight", amount=0.3)

# Check the result of pruning

print(model.fc.weight)
```

9.3 Knowledge Distillation

Knowledge distillation is a technique used to transfer knowledge from a large, complex model (often called the **teacher**) to a smaller, more efficient model (the **student**). The teacher model is typically trained on a large dataset and has high accuracy, while the student model is much smaller, designed to be faster and more memory-efficient.

During the distillation process, the teacher model's predictions are used as soft targets to train the student model. Rather than simply using hard labels (such as class labels), the student model learns to mimic the teacher's output distribution, including its confidence on each prediction. This enables the smaller student model to capture the knowledge of the larger model without having to replicate the full complexity of the teacher network.

The advantage of knowledge distillation is that it allows for the deployment of a more compact and faster model while maintaining a performance level close to that of the larger, more complex model. It is especially useful when there is a need to deploy deep learning models on resource-limited devices, such as smartphones or embedded systems, while still requiring the high performance provided by a larger model.

Code Example: Knowledge Distillation in PyTorch

```python
Python
import torch
```

```python
import torch.nn as nn

import torch.optim as optim

# Define the "Teacher" model (larger
model)

class TeacherModel(nn.Module):

    def __init__(self):

                        super(TeacherModel,
self).__init__()

        self.fc = nn.Linear(10, 10)

    def forward(self, x):

        return self.fc(x)

# Define the "Student" model (smaller
model)

class StudentModel(nn.Module):

    def __init__(self):

                        super(StudentModel,
self).__init__()
```

```python
        self.fc = nn.Linear(10, 10)

    def forward(self, x):

        return self.fc(x)

# Create instances of the models

teacher = TeacherModel()

student = StudentModel()

# Define the distillation loss function
(e.g., Mean Squared Error)

def            distillation_loss(y_student,
y_teacher, T=1.0, alpha=0.5):

        loss  =  nn.MSELoss()(y_student,
y_teacher) * alpha

    return loss

# Train the Student model with the
Teacher's predictions

teacher.eval()  # Set the teacher model to
evaluation mode
```

```python
inputs = torch.randn(5, 10)

# Get the Teacher's outputs

with torch.no_grad():

    teacher_outputs = teacher(inputs)

# Train the Student model

optimizer                                    =
optim.SGD(student.parameters(), lr=0.01)

student.train()

optimizer.zero_grad()

student_outputs = student(inputs)

loss = distillation_loss(student_outputs,
teacher_outputs)

loss.backward()

optimizer.step()

print(f"Distillation Loss: {loss.item()}")
```

9.4 Distributed Training

Distributed training allows a model to be trained across multiple machines or devices, thus accelerating the training process by splitting the workload. PyTorch provides multiple tools for distributed training, such as `torch.nn.DataParallel` or `torch.nn.parallel.DistributedDataParallel`.

Code Example: Distributed Training in PyTorch

```python
import torch

import torch.nn as nn

import torch.optim as optim

import torch.distributed as dist

from torch.nn.parallel import DistributedDataParallel as DDP

# Set up the distributed environment
```

```python
dist.init_process_group(backend='nccl')

# Create a simple model

class SimpleModel(nn.Module):

    def __init__(self):

                        super(SimpleModel,
self).__init__()

        self.fc = nn.Linear(10, 10)

    def forward(self, x):

        return self.fc(x)

# Create an instance of the model

model                                    =
SimpleModel().to(torch.device("cuda"))

#    Wrap    the    model    in
DistributedDataParallel

model = DDP(model)

# Define the optimizer
```

```python
optimizer = optim.SGD(model.parameters(),
lr=0.01)

# Example data for training

inputs            =            torch.randn(32,
10).to(torch.device("cuda"))

targets           =            torch.randn(32,
10).to(torch.device("cuda"))

# Training on multiple GPUs

for epoch in range(10):

    optimizer.zero_grad()

    outputs = model(inputs)

    loss = nn.MSELoss()(outputs, targets)

    loss.backward()

    optimizer.step()


    if dist.get_rank() == 0:  # Only the
main process prints
```

```
        print(f"Epoch {epoch}, Loss:
{loss.item()}")
```

9.5 Performance Optimization

Optimizing performance can involve various strategies such as leveraging **hardware acceleration**, using **mixed-precision arithmetic**, and optimizing **batch processing**. These strategies help reduce training and inference time, making models more efficient.

Code Example: Mixed Precision Training in PyTorch

```python
Python
from torch.cuda.amp import autocast,
GradScaler

# Enable mixed-precision training

model                                    =
SimpleModel().to(torch.device("cuda"))

optimizer = optim.SGD(model.parameters(),
lr=0.01)
```

```python
scaler = GradScaler()

for epoch in range(10):

    optimizer.zero_grad()

        # Perform the forward pass with
autocast (mixed precision)

    with autocast():

        outputs = model(inputs)

            loss = nn.MSELoss()(outputs,
targets)

    # Backward pass with scaler to manage
gradients

    scaler.scale(loss).backward()

    scaler.step(optimizer)

    scaler.update()

        print(f"Epoch   {epoch},   Loss:
{loss.item()}")
```

9.6 Memory Management

Efficient memory management ensures that a model can run effectively even on devices with limited resources. Techniques such as **gradient checkpointing** and **dynamic memory allocation** help reduce memory consumption during training and inference.

Code Example: Gradient Checkpointing in PyTorch

```python
Python
import torch

from torch.utils.checkpoint import checkpoint

# Define a function for checkpointing

def checkpointed_model(x):

    return checkpoint(model, x)

# Create the model and pass the data
through checkpointing
```

```
inputs              =           torch.randn(32,
10).to(torch.device("cuda"))

outputs = checkpointed_model(inputs)
```

This code utilizes **checkpointing**, which reduces memory usage during training by recomputing activations only when necessary.

Model optimization is a crucial part of deploying deep learning models efficiently. With techniques like quantization, pruning, knowledge distillation, distributed training, performance optimization, and memory management, it is possible to make models faster and more efficient without sacrificing accuracy. These techniques are essential for ensuring that AI applications can run efficiently across a wide range of devices and platforms.

Part 4: Production and Deployment

Chapter 10:

Production-Ready PyTorch

In the world of deep learning, it's not enough to simply build an accurate model during the development phase. The true value comes from deploying these models to production environments where they can handle real-world data and provide actionable insights or predictions. PyTorch, being a flexible and dynamic framework, offers a variety of tools and strategies to facilitate the deployment of machine learning models, making them efficient, scalable, and ready for production use.

This chapter will explore various strategies for making a PyTorch model production-ready, including model serving strategies, TorchScript, ONNX integration, mobile deployment, cloud deployment, and model monitoring and maintenance. Each of these components plays a vital role in ensuring that a model operates seamlessly once it is released to production.

10.1 Model Serving Strategies

Model serving is the process of making a trained machine learning model accessible for real-time inference. It involves setting up an endpoint where the model can receive input, perform predictions, and return results to users or other systems. In production, the efficiency and scalability of serving models are paramount.

One common way to serve PyTorch models is by using **RESTful APIs**. These APIs act as intermediaries between the trained model and users or other services. Typically, a model is wrapped inside a server application using frameworks like **Flask** or **FastAPI**. These servers listen for incoming HTTP requests, process the input data, pass it through the model, and return the model's predictions.

To efficiently serve large models or handle a high volume of inference requests, it's often beneficial to use containerized environments like **Docker** and orchestration platforms such as **Kubernetes**. These tools allow for scalable and resilient model deployment, ensuring that the system can handle large amounts of concurrent requests and manage resource allocation effectively.

Code Example: Serving a Model with FastAPI

Here's an example of how to serve a PyTorch model using FastAPI:

```Python
from fastapi import FastAPI

import torch

from pydantic import BaseModel

from typing import List

import torch.nn as nn

# Define a simple model for demonstration

class SimpleModel(nn.Module):

    def __init__(self):

                        super(SimpleModel,
self).__init__()

        self.fc = nn.Linear(10, 1)

    def forward(self, x):

        return self.fc(x)

# Initialize FastAPI and load the model

app = FastAPI()

model = SimpleModel()
```

```python
model.load_state_dict(torch.load("simple_m
odel.pth"))

model.eval()

class Item(BaseModel):

    features: List[float]

@app.post("/predict/")

async def predict(item: Item):

    # Convert input to tensor

                        input_tensor       =
torch.tensor(item.features).float().unsque
eze(0)

    # Perform prediction

    with torch.no_grad():

        prediction = model(input_tensor)

            # Return prediction as a JSON
response
```

```
                    return     {"prediction":
 prediction.item()}
```

In this code, we create a simple neural network model and expose an endpoint `/predict/` that accepts feature data, makes predictions, and returns the result.

10.2 TorchScript

TorchScript is an intermediate representation of a PyTorch model that allows for running the model in a non-Python environment, making it ideal for production. It is particularly useful when the model needs to be deployed in environments that do not support Python, such as mobile devices, embedded systems, or high-performance servers.

TorchScript is designed to convert PyTorch code into a statically typed form that is optimized for speed and can be run independently of the Python runtime. The two main ways to create a TorchScript model are **tracing** and **scripting**.

Tracing involves recording the operations that occur in the forward pass of the model. While this method is fast, it can struggle with models that contain dynamic control flows, such as loops or conditionals. **Scripting**, on the other hand, allows for the conversion of a PyTorch model into TorchScript by analyzing the Python code itself, which can handle dynamic control flows.

Code Example: Converting a Model to TorchScript

```python
Python
import torch

# Define a simple model

class SimpleModel(torch.nn.Module):

    def __init__(self):

                        super(SimpleModel,
self).__init__()

        self.fc = torch.nn.Linear(10, 1)

    def forward(self, x):

        return self.fc(x)

# Create a model instance

model = SimpleModel()
```

```
# Convert the model to TorchScript via
tracing

example_input = torch.randn(1, 10)

traced_model   =   torch.jit.trace(model,
example_input)

# Save the TorchScript model

traced_model.save("traced_model.pt")
```

In this code, we convert a simple model into TorchScript using the `torch.jit.trace` method. The traced model can then be deployed in non-Python environments.

10.3 ONNX Integration

The **Open Neural Network Exchange (ONNX)** is an open format designed to facilitate the interchange of models between different frameworks. PyTorch provides support for exporting models to the ONNX format, allowing users to take a PyTorch model and run it in other deep learning frameworks like **TensorFlow**, **Caffe2**, and **MXNet**. ONNX also enables deployment to a wide range of hardware accelerators, including GPUs, CPUs, and specialized chips like TPUs.

The process of exporting a PyTorch model to ONNX involves converting the model's computation graph into the ONNX format, which can then be optimized and executed by other frameworks or on hardware with specific support for ONNX. This makes the model portable and increases its flexibility across different environments.

Code Example: Exporting a PyTorch Model to ONNX

```python
Python
import torch.onnx

# Define a simple model

class SimpleModel(torch.nn.Module):

    def __init__(self):

                    super(SimpleModel,
self).__init__()

        self.fc = torch.nn.Linear(10, 1)
```

```python
    def forward(self, x):

        return self.fc(x)

# Create model instance

model = SimpleModel()

# Set the model to evaluation mode

model.eval()

# Define example input

example_input = torch.randn(1, 10)

# Export the model to ONNX format

torch.onnx.export(model,    example_input,
"simple_model.onnx", verbose=True)
```

This code snippet demonstrates how to export a simple PyTorch model to the ONNX format, making it compatible with other frameworks and deployment environments.

10.4 Mobile Deployment

Deploying deep learning models on mobile devices (iOS and Android) is becoming increasingly important. PyTorch provides **PyTorch Mobile**, a library that enables the deployment of PyTorch models on mobile devices. With PyTorch Mobile, you can leverage pre-trained models or models that are fine-tuned specifically for mobile, providing efficient inference on smartphones and other mobile devices.

To deploy a model to mobile, you first convert the model to TorchScript. Then, you use PyTorch Mobile's APIs to integrate the model into your mobile application, where it can be used for inference.

Code Example: Deploying a Model to Mobile

To deploy a PyTorch model to a mobile device, you first need to save and load the model in TorchScript format:

```python
import torch

import torch.jit

# Define a simple model

class SimpleModel(torch.nn.Module):

    def __init__(self):
```

```python
                    super(SimpleModel,
self).__init__()

        self.fc = torch.nn.Linear(10, 1)

    def forward(self, x):

        return self.fc(x)

# Convert the model to TorchScript

model = SimpleModel()

example_input = torch.randn(1, 10)

traced_model   =   torch.jit.trace(model,
example_input)

# Save the TorchScript model

traced_model.save("simple_model.pt")
```

Once the model is saved in TorchScript format, you can integrate it into your Android or iOS application using the respective PyTorch Mobile SDKs.

10.5 Cloud Deployment

Cloud deployment involves hosting machine learning models on cloud platforms like **AWS**, **Google Cloud**, or **Microsoft Azure**. These platforms offer scalable infrastructure, allowing you to deploy models and make them available to users via API endpoints. Cloud platforms also provide additional services, such as automated scaling, monitoring, and model versioning.

To deploy a PyTorch model in the cloud, you would typically use Docker to containerize the model along with the necessary libraries. Then, the model is deployed in a serverless or managed Kubernetes environment to handle scaling.

Code Example: Cloud Deployment with Docker

First, create a Dockerfile to containerize your FastAPI application serving the PyTorch model:

```
Unset
# Start from a Python image

FROM python:3.8-slim

# Install dependencies
```

```
RUN pip install fastapi uvicorn torch

# Copy the model and application files

COPY . /app

# Expose the port

EXPOSE 8000

# Run the FastAPI server

CMD ["uvicorn", "main:app", "--host",
"0.0.0.0", "--port", "8000"]
```

Next, build and run the Docker container:

```
Unset
docker build -t pytorch_model_server .

docker run -p 8000:8000 pytorch_model_server
```

This sets up a simple model serving API inside a Docker
container that can be deployed to any cloud platform.

10.6 Model Monitoring and Maintenance

Once a model is deployed to production, it's essential to monitor its performance over time. **Model drift** can occur when the data distribution shifts, causing the model's accuracy to degrade. Regular monitoring ensures that the model continues to provide high-quality predictions and remains aligned with the evolving data.

Tools like **Prometheus**, **Grafana**, and **TensorBoard** can be used to track metrics like response time, prediction accuracy, and system resource usage. When performance degradation is detected, retraining or fine-tuning the model might be necessary.

Code Example: Monitoring with Prometheus

To integrate a model with Prometheus, you would expose metrics (like inference time) via an HTTP endpoint and then use Prometheus to scrape those metrics:

```python
Python
from        prometheus_client       import
start_http_server, Summary

import time
```

```python
# Create a metric to track inference time

INFERENCE_TIME                                    =
Summary('inference_time_seconds',        'Time
spent on inference')

# Define a FastAPI endpoint to serve the
model

@app.post("/predict/")

async def predict(item: Item):

    start_time = time.time()

                        input_tensor        =
torch.tensor(item.features).float().unsque
eze(0)

    # Perform prediction

    with torch.no_grad():

        prediction = model(input_tensor)

        # Record the inference time

    INFERENCE_TIME.observe(time.time() -
start_time)
```

```
                    return  {"prediction":
prediction.item()}

# Start the Prometheus server

start_http_server(8001)
```

This setup tracks the inference time and exposes it to Prometheus for monitoring.

PyTorch provides robust tools and libraries for making machine learning models production-ready. By leveraging strategies like model serving, TorchScript, ONNX integration, and deployment to mobile or cloud platforms, you can ensure that your models are scalable, efficient, and easily accessible. Furthermore, monitoring and maintaining the models in production is crucial for their continued success, enabling businesses to derive consistent value from their AI systems.

Chapter 11: Best Practices and Design Patterns

When working on deep learning projects, particularly with frameworks like PyTorch, it is crucial to adopt effective practices that not only enhance the quality of the code but also promote scalability, reproducibility, and maintainability. In this chapter, we will explore several best practices and design patterns for building robust, efficient, and production-ready PyTorch models. This includes strategies for organizing code, testing models, tracking experiments, managing version control for machine learning projects, documenting code, and collaborating effectively within teams.

11.1 Code Organization

The way code is organized in a machine learning project plays a critical role in its maintainability and scalability. A well-structured codebase helps to ensure that the project is easy to understand, extend, and debug, especially as the complexity of models and the size of the team grow. One common practice is to separate the code into modules that each serve a distinct purpose. This includes directories for data preprocessing, model definitions, training scripts, evaluation, and utility functions. For example, a typical structure might look like this:

```
Unset
project/
├── data/
|   ├── preprocess.py
|   ├── load_data.py
├── models/
|   ├── resnet.py
|   ├── cnn.py
├── training/
|   ├── train.py
|   ├── evaluate.py
├── utils/
|   ├── logger.py
|   ├── helper.py
├── main.py
```

In this structure, the `data` folder contains scripts related to data loading and preprocessing, `models` holds the different neural network architectures, `training` contains the logic for training and evaluating models, and `utils` stores utility functions. Keeping these responsibilities separated allows you to modify or extend specific aspects of the project without affecting the rest of the codebase.

Additionally, it's important to adopt a consistent naming convention for variables, functions, and class names. This promotes readability and makes it easier for other developers to collaborate on the project.

11.2 Testing PyTorch Models

Testing is an often overlooked, yet essential, aspect of deep learning workflows. When training models in PyTorch, you should ensure that your code behaves as expected by writing unit tests. While testing models can be more challenging than testing traditional software due to the stochastic nature of training and the complexity of neural networks, certain aspects can still be tested effectively.

One critical area to test is the model's architecture, ensuring that it is built correctly with the appropriate layers, dimensions, and activation functions. PyTorch provides simple ways to inspect model outputs and gradients to verify that they behave as expected. Additionally, testing the training and evaluation pipelines is essential. For instance, you can write tests to ensure that the optimizer updates parameters during training or that the model produces reasonable outputs.

Here's an example of testing a model's forward pass in PyTorch:

```python
import torch

import pytest

from models.resnet import ResNet

def test_resnet_forward_pass():

    model = ResNet()

    # Create a random tensor simulating a
    batch of images (e.g., 8 images, 3
    channels, 224x224)

    x = torch.randn(8, 3, 224, 224)

    # Perform a forward pass

    output = model(x)
```

```
# Test if the output has the expected
shape
    assert output.shape == (8, 1000)   #
assuming 1000 output classes
```

In this test, we check if the forward pass of a ResNet model produces the correct output shape for a given input tensor. This is a simple but effective way to ensure that the model architecture is correctly implemented.

11.3 Logging and Experiment Tracking

In machine learning projects, especially when training large models, tracking the progress of experiments is crucial. Logging and experiment tracking allow you to monitor important metrics such as loss, accuracy, hyperparameters, and training duration, ensuring reproducibility and providing insights into model performance over time.

PyTorch doesn't provide built-in experiment tracking, but there are several excellent third-party libraries that integrate seamlessly with it, such as **TensorBoard** and

Weights & Biases. TensorBoard allows you to visualize training progress, model architecture, and other metrics in real time. You can log metrics like loss and accuracy, as well as visualize model weights and gradients. For more advanced tracking, tools like **Weights & Biases** offer features like hyperparameter optimization, version control for experiments, and collaborative features for teams.

Here's how you can integrate TensorBoard with PyTorch:

```python
Python
from torch.utils.tensorboard import SummaryWriter

# Create a SummaryWriter instance

writer = SummaryWriter()

# Log scalar values (e.g., loss)

for epoch in range(num_epochs):

    writer.add_scalar('Loss/train', loss, epoch)

    writer.add_scalar('Accuracy/train', accuracy, epoch)

# Visualize model graph
```

```
sample_input = torch.randn(1, 3, 224, 224)

writer.add_graph(model, sample_input)

# Close the writer

writer.close()
```

In this example, we log the training loss and accuracy at each epoch. Additionally, we log the model architecture using `add_graph`, which is useful for understanding and debugging complex networks.

11.4 Version Control for ML

Version control is essential for managing machine learning projects, especially when multiple team members are working on different aspects of the code. Git, the most commonly used version control system, helps you manage code changes and collaborate effectively by maintaining a history of changes and enabling you to revert to previous versions when necessary.

In machine learning projects, it's also important to track changes in models, datasets, and hyperparameters. Tools like **DVC (Data Version Control)** extend Git to handle large datasets and models by allowing you to version control not only the code but also data and machine learning artifacts.

For instance, if you are working on a model and change hyperparameters, you can use DVC to track those changes:

```
Unset
# Initialize DVC

dvc init

# Add a dataset to DVC

dvc add data/train.csv

# Commit the changes to Git and DVC

git add data/train.csv.dvc

git commit -m "Added training data"

# Push changes to remote storage

dvc push
```

In this example, we track changes to the dataset and store them using DVC, which integrates seamlessly with Git.

11.5 Documentation

Good documentation is essential for any project, and machine learning projects are no exception. Documentation helps team members understand how to use, extend, and maintain the code. It also ensures that new contributors can quickly get up to speed.

For PyTorch models, you should document your classes, methods, and functions clearly, specifying input/output formats, expected behavior, and any assumptions made during implementation. Tools like **Sphinx** can be used to generate API documentation from docstrings, and **Markdown** files can provide high-level descriptions of the project, goals, and setup instructions.

A simple docstring example for a model class in PyTorch might look like this:

```Python
class SimpleCNN(nn.Module):

    """
```

A simple Convolutional Neural Network for image classification.

Attributes:

conv1 (nn.Conv2d): First convolutional layer.

conv2 (nn.Conv2d): Second convolutional layer.

fc1 (nn.Linear): Fully connected layer.

fc2 (nn.Linear): Final output layer.

Methods:

forward(x): Performs a forward pass through the network.

```
    """

    def __init__(self):

        super(SimpleCNN, self).__init__()
```

```python
        self.conv1 = nn.Conv2d(1, 32,
kernel_size=3)

        self.conv2 = nn.Conv2d(32, 64,
kernel_size=3)

        self.fc1 = nn.Linear(64 * 6 * 6,
128)

        self.fc2 = nn.Linear(128, 10)

    def forward(self, x):

        """

        Forward pass through the network.

        Args:

            x (Tensor): Input image tensor
of shape (batch_size, 1, 28, 28).

        Returns:

            Tensor: Output tensor of shape
(batch_size, 10) representing class
scores.

        """
```

```
x = torch.relu(self.conv1(x))

x = torch.relu(self.conv2(x))

x = x.view(x.size(0), -1)

x = torch.relu(self.fc1(x))

return self.fc2(x)
```

In this example, the docstring provides an overview of the SimpleCNN class, describing its attributes and methods. Each function also includes details about the arguments it accepts and the return values, helping other developers or users understand the function's purpose.

11.6 Collaboration in Teams

Collaboration is key to the success of any machine learning project, and this is especially true in large teams working on complex tasks. Communication between team members should be facilitated through version control systems like Git, project management tools like Jira or Trello, and regular meetings or communication channels.

When working in a team, it's important to establish coding standards and workflows to avoid conflicts. Code reviews should be a standard part of the development process to ensure that the code adheres to best practices and is of high quality. In addition, clear guidelines should be set for branching and merging code in version control systems, ensuring that everyone works efficiently without overwriting each other's work.

Tools like **Jupyter Notebooks** or **Google Colab** can also be used to collaborate on experiments and share results interactively, making it easier for teams to iterate quickly and test different approaches.

Adopting best practices in PyTorch and machine learning projects ensures that the code is clean, maintainable, and scalable. By focusing on code organization, testing, logging, version control, documentation, and collaboration, you can enhance the productivity of your team and create high-quality models that are easier to deploy and maintain. Following these practices will allow you to build robust, reproducible machine learning workflows and create more efficient and effective models.

Chapter 12: Case Studies and Advanced Projects

Developing deep learning models with PyTorch goes beyond simple experimentation in controlled environments. This chapter delves into practical applications, industrial workflows, performance optimization techniques, and production deployment strategies. You will learn how to approach complete projects from data acquisition to deployment and maintenance while tackling complex challenges in real-world scenarios.

12.1   Real-World   Implementation Examples

To understand how PyTorch is applied in practice, it is crucial to examine real-world examples. One of the most representative use cases is deep learning for medical image analysis. Convolutional Neural Networks (CNNs) have been trained on large radiology datasets to detect abnormalities such as tumors or lung diseases. These models have improved diagnostic accuracy and reduced the workload for medical professionals.

Another major application is Natural Language Processing (NLP) in the financial sector. Transformers such as BERT are used to analyze legal documents, detect fraud, and enhance decision-making processes. These models have significantly reduced the time required to process large volumes of text while improving accuracy in text classification and entity recognition.

In e-commerce, PyTorch plays a key role in building personalized recommendation systems. Companies like Amazon and Alibaba use Recurrent Neural Networks (RNNs) and embeddings to analyze shopping patterns and suggest highly relevant products. These models not only enhance user experience but also drive higher conversion rates and customer lifetime value.

12.2 Industry-Specific Applications

Each industry has unique challenges that require specialized deep learning solutions. In the automotive sector, CNNs and Transformer-based models are integral to autonomous vehicle development. These models process real-time data from multiple sensors, cameras, and radars to make safe and efficient driving decisions.

In the entertainment industry, PyTorch has been used for content generation through Generative Adversarial

Networks (GANs). Video game and film companies leverage GANs to create realistic characters, animations, and visual effects. The ability to generate high-quality content has transformed the way digital media is produced.

Another major sector benefiting from PyTorch is biotechnology. Deep learning models have accelerated drug discovery by simulating molecular interactions. Graph Neural Networks (GNNs) analyze chemical structures and predict drug effectiveness, reducing the time required for pharmaceutical research and development.

12.3 End-to-End Project Workflows

Building a deep learning project in PyTorch involves multiple essential phases, from data acquisition to model deployment and monitoring. A typical workflow consists of the following steps:

1. **Problem Definition and Data Collection**: Identifying the model's objective—whether classification, regression, or generation—and gathering appropriate datasets. The quality and quantity of data are crucial for the model's success.

2. **Data Preprocessing**: Cleaning and transforming data for efficient neural network processing. Techniques such as normalization, outlier removal,

and data augmentation are applied depending on the problem.

3. **Model Architecture Design**: Choosing the right architecture is critical. Pretrained models like ResNet or EfficientNet can be used for computer vision, BERT for NLP, or custom architectures for specific tasks.

4. **Model Training**: Defining the loss function and selecting appropriate optimizers such as Adam or SGD. Transfer learning and regularization techniques like dropout can improve model generalization.

5. **Evaluation and Fine-Tuning**: Assessing model performance using metrics like accuracy, recall, and F1-score. Hyperparameter tuning is crucial for optimizing performance.

6. **Production Deployment**: Trained models can be exported using TorchScript or converted to formats like ONNX for integration into servers, mobile applications, or cloud environments.

7. **Monitoring and Maintenance**: Once deployed, the model must be continuously monitored to detect performance degradation and adapt to new data.

12.4 Performance Optimization Case Studies

Optimizing deep learning models is essential for reducing training time and improving efficiency in production. One widely used technique is quantization, which reduces the numerical precision of model weights without significantly impacting accuracy. In computer vision applications, quantization has enabled CNNs to run efficiently on mobile devices.

Another crucial technique is pruning, which removes unnecessary connections in neural networks, reducing model size and speeding up inference. Studies have shown that networks like ResNet can be significantly compressed without sacrificing performance in image classification.

Additionally, distributed training on multiple GPUs or cloud computing clusters has enabled the scaling of large models. PyTorch Distributed makes it easier to implement techniques like data-parallel training and gradient accumulation for efficient resource utilization.

12.5 Debugging Complex Models

Training deep learning models often presents challenges such as overfitting, slow convergence, or unstable learning. One effective debugging technique is visualizing gradients and activation distributions to detect imbalances in information propagation.

Tools like TensorBoard and PyTorch Lightning facilitate the inspection of layer behavior in neural networks. Additionally, techniques like gradient clipping help stabilize training in deep architectures such as Transformers, preventing exploding gradients from disrupting optimization.

12.6 Production Deployment Stories

Deploying deep learning models in production environments comes with various challenges. Companies like Facebook and OpenAI have used TorchScript to convert PyTorch models into optimized versions for real-time inference.

In virtual assistants and recommendation engines, integrating models into cloud services has allowed them to scale to millions of users. E-commerce companies use PyTorch to personalize shopping experiences based on user behavior, improving conversion rates and customer retention.

Finally, in industrial applications, PyTorch-powered quality inspection systems have reduced human error and improved defect detection accuracy. These use cases demonstrate that PyTorch is not only a powerful research tool but also a practical solution for real-world deployment.

Appendices

Appendix A: PyTorch Ecosystem

PyTorch is more than just a deep learning framework—it is an entire ecosystem designed to support researchers, engineers, and developers in building and deploying machine learning models. This appendix explores the various libraries, tools, and community-driven resources that make PyTorch a powerful and flexible choice for artificial intelligence applications. Additionally, it highlights key research contributions that have influenced PyTorch's evolution and its adoption in academia and industry.

Popular PyTorch Libraries

The PyTorch ecosystem includes a wide range of specialized libraries designed for different machine learning domains.

One of the most widely used libraries is **TorchVision**, which provides datasets, pre-trained models, and utilities for computer vision tasks such as image classification, object detection, and image segmentation. It includes popular datasets like ImageNet and COCO, along with implementations of state-of-the-art architectures such as ResNet, VGG, and EfficientNet.

For natural language processing (NLP), **TorchText** offers efficient tools for text preprocessing, tokenization, and dataset management. It simplifies working with large-scale text data by providing built-in datasets, vocabulary management utilities, and integration with popular embedding models like GloVe and FastText.

TorchAudio is designed for audio and speech processing applications. It includes data loaders for common audio datasets, pre-trained speech recognition models, and utilities for waveform transformations such as spectrogram generation and Mel-frequency cepstral coefficient (MFCC) extraction. PyTorch-based speech models, such as Wav2Vec and DeepSpeech, benefit from TorchAudio's seamless integration with the core PyTorch framework.

For reinforcement learning, **TorchRL** provides modular and efficient components for developing RL algorithms. It includes implementations of fundamental algorithms like Deep Q-Networks (DQN), Proximal Policy Optimization (PPO), and Advantage Actor-Critic (A2C), along with tools for training agents in simulated environments.

Another important library is **TorchRec**, which is optimized for large-scale recommendation systems. It provides distributed training support for collaborative filtering models and deep learning-based recommendation architectures used in personalized content delivery platforms.

Tools and Frameworks

PyTorch offers various tools that enhance model training, optimization, and deployment.

PyTorch Lightning simplifies training by structuring code into reusable modules, making experiments more organized and scalable. It abstracts away much of the boilerplate code associated with PyTorch training loops, enabling efficient multi-GPU and TPU training.

For hyperparameter optimization, **Optuna** is a powerful tool that integrates seamlessly with PyTorch. It allows users to automate hyperparameter tuning using techniques like Bayesian optimization, grid search, and evolutionary algorithms to improve model performance.

When it comes to deploying models in production, **TorchScript** is a core tool that allows PyTorch models to be serialized and optimized for inference. It converts dynamic models into a more static, optimized representation, making them more efficient for deployment in real-time systems. Additionally, **ONNX (Open Neural**

Network Exchange) provides interoperability between PyTorch and other frameworks, enabling seamless model export for inference in TensorFlow, CoreML, or specialized hardware accelerators.

For large-scale distributed training, **Torch Distributed** provides robust support for training models across multiple GPUs and compute nodes. It includes implementations of distributed data parallelism (DDP) and pipeline parallelism, making it ideal for scaling deep learning workloads.

Another significant tool is **TorchServe**, which streamlines model serving by providing an easy-to-use framework for deploying trained PyTorch models as RESTful APIs. It supports features such as batch inference, model versioning, and multi-model deployment, making it an essential tool for bringing PyTorch models into production.

Community Resources

The PyTorch community is one of its greatest strengths, providing extensive support through forums, documentation, and open-source contributions.

The **PyTorch Discussion Forum** serves as a central hub for developers to ask questions, share ideas, and collaborate on projects. It covers topics ranging from beginner-level troubleshooting to advanced research discussions.

GitHub repositories for PyTorch and its associated libraries contain open-source implementations of models, tutorials, and research papers. Developers frequently contribute improvements and report issues, making PyTorch one of the most actively maintained deep learning frameworks.

For learning and education, **PyTorch Tutorials** provide step-by-step guides covering fundamental concepts, model implementations, and advanced topics such as reinforcement learning and generative adversarial networks (GANs). These tutorials are maintained by both the PyTorch development team and the broader community.

PyTorch also has an active presence on platforms like **Reddit, Stack Overflow, and Twitter**, where developers share insights, discuss new research, and provide solutions to common challenges.

To facilitate collaboration in machine learning research, **PyTorch Conferences and Meetups** are regularly organized by the community. Events such as PyTorch Developer Day and PyTorch Global Summits bring together researchers and practitioners to discuss the latest advancements and use cases.

Research Papers and References

PyTorch has been widely adopted in academic research due to its flexibility and ease of use. Some of the most influential research papers that have utilized PyTorch include:

- **"Attention Is All You Need"** (2017) – The groundbreaking paper that introduced the Transformer architecture, which has become the foundation of modern NLP models like BERT and GPT.

- **"Deep Residual Learning for Image Recognition"** (2015) – Introduced ResNet, a deep CNN architecture that significantly improved image classification performance.

- **"BERT: Pre-training of Deep Bidirectional Transformers for Language Understanding"** (2018) – Introduced BERT, a model that revolutionized NLP by leveraging bidirectional self-attention mechanisms.

- **"AlphaGo Zero: Mastering the Game of Go Without Human Knowledge"** (2017) – Demonstrated reinforcement learning capabilities using deep neural networks trained with PyTorch.

- **"EfficientNet: Rethinking Model Scaling for Convolutional Neural Networks"** (2019) – Proposed a novel approach to scaling CNN architectures, achieving state-of-the-art performance with fewer parameters.

Additionally, PyTorch has been referenced in thousands of academic papers across fields such as medical imaging, robotics, computational biology, and astrophysics. Its widespread adoption in research has led to continuous improvements and new features that cater to cutting-edge AI developments.

Appendix B: Mathematics for Deep Learning

Deep learning models are built upon a strong mathematical foundation, with concepts from linear algebra, calculus, probability, and optimization playing crucial roles in their development and training. Understanding these mathematical principles is essential for grasping how neural networks learn from data, optimize parameters, and make predictions. This appendix provides an overview of the key mathematical concepts used in deep learning and their applications within the PyTorch framework.

Linear Algebra Refresher

Linear algebra forms the backbone of deep learning, as neural networks primarily operate on multidimensional arrays known as tensors. At the core of linear algebra are **vectors**, **matrices**, and **tensor operations**, which facilitate computations such as transformations, projections, and optimization in high-dimensional spaces.

A **vector** is a one-dimensional array of numbers representing points in space, often used to store features in machine learning. A **matrix** is a two-dimensional array where each row and column holds numerical values, commonly used to represent datasets, transformation functions, and weight matrices in neural networks. More generally, a **tensor** extends this concept to higher dimensions, allowing for the representation of multi-channel images, sequential data, and complex model parameters.

Matrix operations such as **dot products**, **matrix multiplication**, and **eigenvalue decomposition** are fundamental to deep learning. The dot product measures similarity between two vectors, while matrix multiplication enables transformations in neural network layers. Eigenvalue decomposition and **singular value decomposition (SVD)** play key roles in techniques like **principal component analysis (PCA)**, which is used for dimensionality reduction.

In PyTorch, tensors are created and manipulated using the `torch.Tensor` class, which supports essential operations such as addition, multiplication, transposition, and reshaping. Efficient implementation of matrix operations ensures that deep learning computations are optimized for performance, especially when leveraging GPUs.

Calculus Concepts

Calculus is crucial for understanding how deep learning models optimize their parameters through differentiation and integration. At the heart of this process is **gradient descent**, which relies on derivatives to adjust model weights and minimize errors.

A function's **derivative** represents the rate of change, providing information about how small changes in input affect the output. In deep learning, the **gradient** of the loss function with respect to model parameters guides weight updates during training. The gradient is computed using **partial derivatives**, as each parameter contributes to the overall loss.

PyTorch automates gradient computation through its **autograd** module, which performs **automatic differentiation**. The **chain rule** plays a critical role in this process, allowing for the computation of gradients in multi-layer neural networks by propagating derivatives backward through each layer, a process known as **backpropagation**.

Another essential calculus concept is **convex optimization**, which ensures that gradient-based algorithms converge toward an optimal solution. While deep learning loss functions are often non-convex, understanding convexity helps in selecting appropriate optimization techniques and avoiding local minima during training.

Probability and Statistics

Deep learning models operate under uncertainty, making probability and statistics essential for tasks like classification, generative modeling, and reinforcement learning.

Probability distributions describe the likelihood of different outcomes, with common distributions including the **Gaussian (normal) distribution**, **Bernoulli distribution**, and **multinomial distribution**. The Gaussian distribution is particularly important in deep learning, as many optimization techniques and regularization strategies assume normally distributed data.

Bayesian principles also influence deep learning through techniques like **Bayesian neural networks**, which model uncertainty in predictions. **Conditional probability** and **Bayes' theorem** are used in applications such as **Naive Bayes classifiers** and **Bayesian optimization**.

Entropy measures uncertainty in a distribution, while **cross-entropy loss** is widely used in classification problems to compare predicted probabilities with actual labels. **Kullback-Leibler (KL) divergence** quantifies the difference between two probability distributions and is commonly applied in variational autoencoders (VAEs) and generative adversarial networks (GANs).

In PyTorch, probabilistic models are implemented using the `torch.distributions` module, which provides tools for sampling, estimating probability density functions, and computing loss functions for probabilistic models.

Optimization Theory

Optimization is the process of minimizing a model's loss function to achieve better performance. The most commonly used optimization algorithm in deep learning is **gradient descent**, which iteratively updates model parameters in the direction of negative gradients to reduce loss.

There are several variations of gradient descent:

- **Batch Gradient Descent:** Computes the gradient using the entire dataset, leading to stable but computationally expensive updates.

- **Stochastic Gradient Descent (SGD):** Updates weights based on individual data points, introducing noise but allowing for faster convergence.

- **Mini-batch Gradient Descent:** Strikes a balance between efficiency and stability by computing updates on small batches of data.

Several advanced optimization techniques improve upon standard gradient descent by adjusting the learning rate dynamically. **Momentum-based optimizers** such as **SGD with momentum** help accelerate convergence by incorporating past gradients. **Adaptive optimizers** like **Adam, RMSprop, and Adagrad** adjust learning rates based on past gradient magnitudes, enabling more efficient learning in complex deep networks.

Regularization techniques like **L1 and L2 regularization (weight decay)**, **dropout**, and **batch normalization** help prevent overfitting and improve generalization. These methods control model complexity by either penalizing large weight values or introducing noise during training.

PyTorch provides a range of built-in optimizers in the `torch.optim` module, allowing users to experiment with different learning strategies to achieve optimal performance.

Appendix C: Hardware Considerations

Deep learning workloads demand significant computational resources, and selecting the right hardware plays a crucial role in the efficiency and speed of model training. PyTorch is designed to leverage high-performance computing resources, particularly GPUs, to accelerate deep learning tasks. Understanding hardware considerations, including GPU selection, CPU vs. GPU training, multi-GPU setups, and cloud computing options, is essential for optimizing deep learning workflows.

GPU Selection Guide

Graphics Processing Units (GPUs) have revolutionized deep learning by enabling massively parallel computations. Unlike Central Processing Units (CPUs), which are optimized for sequential processing, GPUs excel at handling large-scale matrix operations, making them ideal for deep learning workloads.

When selecting a GPU for PyTorch-based deep learning, several factors should be considered:

- **CUDA Support**: NVIDIA GPUs with CUDA (Compute Unified Device Architecture) support are the preferred choice for PyTorch due to their compatibility with PyTorch's GPU-accelerated libraries. AMD GPUs are gaining PyTorch support with ROCm, but NVIDIA remains the dominant choice.

- **Memory Capacity (VRAM)**: Deep learning models, particularly large-scale neural networks, require substantial GPU memory. For tasks such as training large transformer models, GPUs with 24GB or more of VRAM, such as the NVIDIA RTX 3090, RTX 4090, A100, or H100, are recommended.

- **Tensor Cores**: Modern GPUs, such as NVIDIA's RTX and A-series GPUs, come equipped with Tensor Cores, specialized hardware that accelerates mixed-precision deep learning computations. These significantly improve training efficiency while maintaining model accuracy.

- **Bandwidth and Compute Performance**: The GPU's memory bandwidth and Floating Point Operations Per Second (FLOPS) determine how quickly it can process deep learning workloads. High-performance GPUs with higher FLOPS and memory bandwidth perform better on complex models.

For beginners, consumer-grade GPUs like the NVIDIA RTX 3060, 3070, or 4060 offer a balance between affordability and performance. For enterprise-scale AI applications, workstation and data-center GPUs such as the NVIDIA A100, H100, and L40S are preferred due to their superior memory capacity and computational power.

CPU vs. GPU Training

While CPUs can be used for training deep learning models, they are significantly slower compared to GPUs for large-scale computations. CPUs are optimized for general-purpose tasks and sequential processing, making them ideal for data preprocessing and model deployment but less efficient for intensive training tasks.

GPU acceleration offers major advantages for deep learning training:

- **Parallel Processing**: GPUs perform thousands of operations simultaneously, speeding up tasks like matrix multiplications and convolution operations, which are fundamental in deep learning.

- **Optimized Frameworks**: PyTorch is built to take advantage of CUDA-enabled GPUs through libraries like cuDNN, ensuring significant speedups in training and inference.

- **Memory Management**: GPUs handle large batches of data more efficiently, reducing the overhead caused by frequent memory transfers.

Despite GPUs being the preferred choice for training, CPUs remain essential in deep learning pipelines, particularly for data preprocessing, model inference, and running lightweight models in production environments. Intel and AMD high-core-count CPUs, such as Intel Xeon and AMD EPYC, are often used in server and cloud-based deep learning setups.

Multi-GPU Setups

For large-scale training tasks, a single GPU may not be sufficient. Multi-GPU setups enable parallel processing across multiple GPUs, significantly reducing training time for complex models. PyTorch supports multi-GPU training through **data parallelism** and **model parallelism**.

- **Data Parallelism**: In this approach, the model is replicated across multiple GPUs, and each GPU processes a subset of the data. Gradients are averaged and synchronized before updating model parameters. PyTorch's `torch.nn.DataParallel` and `torch.nn.parallel.DistributedDataParallel` (DDP) facilitate multi-GPU training efficiently. DDP is the preferred method as it provides better scalability and performance.

- **Model Parallelism**: When a model is too large to fit on a single GPU, it can be split across multiple GPUs, with different parts of the model residing on different GPUs. This approach is useful for training extremely large models, such as transformer-based architectures.

Multi-GPU training requires high-speed interconnects, such as NVIDIA NVLink or PCIe 4.0, to enable fast communication between GPUs. Additionally, using high-bandwidth memory (HBM) on GPUs like the NVIDIA A100 further improves performance.

Cloud Computing Options

For researchers and developers who lack access to high-end GPUs, cloud computing provides a cost-effective and scalable alternative for deep learning workloads.

Several cloud providers offer GPU instances optimized for deep learning:

- **Google Cloud AI Platform**: Provides access to NVIDIA A100, V100, and T4 GPUs, as well as TPUs (Tensor Processing Units) for accelerating deep learning workloads.

- **AWS (Amazon Web Services)**: Offers EC2 instances with NVIDIA GPUs, including P-series (Tesla V100), G-series (T4), and A-series (A100, H100).

- **Microsoft Azure Machine Learning**: Provides various GPU-powered instances for deep learning model training and deployment.

- **Google Colab**: A free cloud-based Jupyter notebook service that provides access to Tesla T4 GPUs for deep learning experiments, though with usage limitations.

Cloud-based GPU resources enable flexibility, allowing users to scale their compute resources as needed. However, cloud costs can accumulate over time, making on-premise GPU setups a more economical solution for long-term deep learning projects.

Thanks for reading!

Throughout this book, we have explored the core principles and advanced techniques of deep learning using PyTorch. Beginning with fundamental concepts such as tensors, automatic differentiation, and neural network architectures, we progressed through training strategies, evaluation metrics, and optimization techniques. We then delved into specialized applications, including computer vision, natural language processing, and real-world case studies. Additionally, we examined the PyTorch ecosystem, mathematical foundations, and hardware considerations to provide a well-rounded understanding of deep learning workflows.

The goal of this book has been to bridge the gap between theory and practical implementation, enabling readers to confidently build and deploy deep learning models. Whether you are an aspiring machine learning practitioner, a researcher, or an industry professional, mastering PyTorch opens up endless possibilities for innovation. The hands-on examples, best practices, and case studies included in these chapters were designed to equip you with the skills necessary to tackle real-world AI challenges.

To the reader, I sincerely thank you for choosing this book as part of your deep learning journey. I hope that it has provided you with not just knowledge, but also inspiration to explore, experiment, and push the boundaries of AI. PyTorch continues to evolve, and I encourage you to stay engaged with the PyTorch community, contribute to open-source projects, and keep expanding your expertise.

Your time and dedication to learning are greatly appreciated. I hope that this book has delivered maximum value, helping you achieve your goals in deep learning and artificial intelligence. Thank you for your support, and I look forward to seeing the innovative projects you create with PyTorch!

Ethan Westwood

SMART B O O K S

www.ingramcontent.com/pod-product-compliance
Lightning Source LLC
LaVergne TN
LVHW051445050326
832903LV00030BD/3246